EMOTIONAL ABUSE AND TRAUMA RECOVERY

BREAKING FREE FROM ABUSIVE AND TOXIC RELATIONSHIPS BY RECLAIMING YOUR LIFE; GASLIGHTING, MANIPULATION, LYING, NARCISSISTIC ABUSE, AND MORE

CASSANDRA MCBRIDE

CONTENTS

Introduction   5

1. UNDERSTANDING THE REALITY OF EMOTIONAL
   ABUSE   11
   What is Emotional Abuse?   11
   Signs of Abuse   12
   What Causes Someone to Become an Abuser?   17
   Effects of Emotional Abuse   24

2. UNRAVELING ALL THE TACTICS   27
   Covert and Overt Emotional Abuse   28
   Symptoms of Covert Abuse and Getting Assistance   31
   The Narcissistic Personality Disorder (NPD)   33
   Manipulation and Guilt Tripping   35
   Various Guilt Trips   35
   Emotional Abuse Worksheet   46

3. GETTING READY TO SURMOUNT THE
   CHALLENGES   49
   Will an Abuser Just Let You Leave?   49
   Why Leaving May Be Difficult   54
   Get Ready to Surmount Flying Monkeys   57
   Get Ready to Deal with Stalking   61
   Get Ready to Deal with Begging, Guilt Tripping, and
   Playing the Victim   64
   Get Ready To Deal With Your Own Fear of Being Alone   70
   Surmount the Challenges Worksheet   77

4. BREAKING FREE FROM NARCISSISM   79
   What Is Narcissism?   80
   Types of Narcissists   81
   Understanding the Narcissist's Tactics   83
   How To Recognize a Narcissist   85
   Why It Is Difficult to Break Free From a Narcissist   87
   Breaking Free from Narcissism Worksheet   91

5. HOW TO BREAK FREE FROM TOXIC FAMILY RELATIONSHIPS 95
The Rigors of a Dysfunctional Family 95
Recognizing Unhealthy Family Patterns 98
Deciding To Cut Ties With Toxic Family Members 100
Dealing With an Emotionally Abusive/Manipulative Parents 103
Dealing With Emotionally Abusive Siblings and Other Family Members 107
Family Toxic Relationships Worksheet 114

6. EXTREME COURSES OF ACTION 117
Finding Closure with Your Abuser 117
How To Go No-Contact With a Narcissist or an Abuser 118
Co-Parenting With an Abusive Ex-Spouse 120
Safe Co-Parenting With Your Former Abuser 121
Plan a Safety Strategy 124
Extreme Course of Action Worksheet 124

7. WATCH OUT FOR VICTIM SYNDROME 127
What is a Victim Mentality/Syndrome? 128
Signs That You Have Victim Syndrome 130
The Victim, Victimizer, and Rescuer Cycle 131
Self-Pity After Emotional Abuse and Trauma 134
Victim Syndrome Worksheet 136
Yes or No answers needed 136

8. TAKING CARE OF YOURSELF BIG-TIME 139
Self-Compassion and Empathy Are Important 139
Avoid Negative Thought Patterns 140
Self-Care Tips Towards Recovery from Abuse 142
Suicide Prevention 148
Maintain Success on a Personal Level 148
Taking Care of Yourself Worksheet 151

Conclusion 153
References 155

INTRODUCTION

Disbelief. Confusion. Fear. Anxiety. Constant stress. Frozen feelings. Depression. Mental exhaustion. Anger. Heartache. Hopelessness. These are just a few of the emotions expressed by victims of emotional abuse. It takes courage to face painful experiences, and I hope you'll take a moment to be proud of your choice to recover.

"Is it abuse?"

"Am I overreacting?"

"Could it be my fault?"

Victims of emotional abuse are often confused about whether or not their partner's behavior is, in fact, abusive. They may try to explain or confront the problems with their partner, but this often leads to even more disrespectful and manipulative treatment.

This lack of understanding and awareness by others can leave you feeling alone and unsupported. Without the help of someone who has lived through emotional abuse themselves, your journey toward recovery might feel like a lonely, difficult pursuit. This book is intended to show you that you are not alone. Many people have experienced emotional abuse; thankfully, more people are starting to grasp it.

This book intends to help you acknowledge, understand, and recover from emotional abuse. If you are reading this, it's likely because you know something is wrong. You may not know how to describe or define it, but you are looking for answers and help with finding solutions. It is important to understand that healing will be a process, and you can't do it alone.

I myself have had my own personal struggles in this area, growing up with a narcissistic mother and not recognizing the symptoms until later on in life. Furthermore, in my professional life, I've spent years working with individuals and couples who have developed deep psychological issues caused by emotional abuse. Their stories, and the trauma they suffered from, helped facilitate a personal passion of mine. A passion for helping people identify, overcome and recover from these emotional abusers for good.

This book will help you channel the complexities of abuse and recovery into tangible concepts and exercises. As you read through and complete the exercises on these pages, you will uncover the patterns and dynamics of your relationships, identify your strengths and values, discover your resilience, and learn practical strategies to manage daily challenges and promote improved self-worth and well-being.

Research from the field of abuse recovery shows that if you have been emotionally or psychologically abused by a narcissist, manipulator, or bully, the chances are your sense of power, self-esteem, social connectedness, and confidence may have taken a beating.

Thankfully, scientists and mental health professionals working in this field have found patient-centric techniques that can help you recover faster and thrive better by focusing on three things:

- Your self-confidence
- Finding a sense of meaning for what happened to you
- Building supportive, social, or spiritual connections

Emotional abuse, typically in the form of verbal abuse, is a battering that causes no physical bruises, yet it is just as painful, and recovery tends to take a lot longer. When you live as a victim of abuse, your life becomes increasingly confusing. Your abuser may act like one person in public, and then behind closed doors, they become somebody else.

Frequently, there is no other witness for the abused person and nobody else to understand what you have gone through. What's worse is other people in your life may see the abuser as a nice person.

This book is made to help you notice the subtle signs of emotional abuse, and to reveal the slight nuances and reality that this type of abuse can cause. Those who have experienced emotional abuse would much rather forget their past altogether. Everybody would love to forget the bad parts of their past, but we can't. What we can do is learn from those times and make choices now to make sure we have a better future.

If you have been a victim of emotional abuse, I hope this book will lead you in the right direction towards recovery.

Special Bonus

Want These Special Tips & Tricks Guides for Free?

Get **_FREE_** unlimited access to them and all of my new books by joining my fanbase!

Scan with your camera to join!

1

UNDERSTANDING THE REALITY OF EMOTIONAL ABUSE

WHAT IS EMOTIONAL ABUSE?

Emotional abuse is when someone uses their emotions to control, humiliate, shame, accuse, or manipulate another person. A relationship is generally considered emotionally abusive when there is a pattern of abusive remarks and bullying behaviors that impair a person's self-esteem and mental health. This abuse isn't exclusive to romantic relationships either. Emotional abuse can take place in the workplace, between friends, and between family members.

Emotional abuse is one of the most difficult types of abuse to spot, and it might be subtle and underhanded or overt and deceptive. In either case, the victim's self-esteem is eroded, and they begin questioning their views and reality.

It can happen to anyone: children, teens, or adults. Even strong people with a "proper upbringing" and a solid foundation of confidence can enter into an abusive relationship. When someone is finally free of the abuse, they understand something was wrong. Still, during the period of emotional trauma, it can be difficult to see there is another choice besides just accepting what is happening to you.

Just because there is no physical mark does not mean the abuser did not commit a problem or a crime, and it just means most law enforcement agencies are not willing to work as hard to help you prove the trauma and stop it.

As such, emotional abuse is an elusive subject. Even though it can sometimes be invisible to the outside world, it can leave deep scars on a person's mind. The problems that arise from such experiences can fester and become more complicated over the years, causing emotional issues that can manifest themselves in many ways and places. The actual relationship between the abuser and the victim may not always be where the damage ends.

Those who go through abuse, fail to address the problem properly, and let go of the emotional weight can carry it over to their children. If suppressed and allowed to fester, emotional harm can become like a disease that can even be passed down through the generations. Folks can find themselves lashing out. They may not know how to express their love, may have difficulty communicating with loved ones on a meaningful level. They can end up unintentionally harming others - even their children - because of deep-seated, unaddressed problems.

Therefore, if you have ever been a victim of emotional abuse, it is imperative that you fully understand what it is, why it happens, and how you can overcome the problems it has left you with. No matter how difficult it might be to identify and mend the problem, you can and must do it for your own emotional health, and for the sake of your loved ones.

SIGNS OF ABUSE

Are You Going Through Emotional Abuse?

Emotional abuse is defined as an action that diminishes, isolates, humiliates, confines, and verbally assaults a person's self-worth, dignity, and identity. Chronic psychological abuse can lead to anxiety, low self-confidence, personality changes, depression, and even suicide.

Behaviors described in this section focus on power and control tactics. These behaviors are easier to understand when we view them on a continuum instead of as entirely good or bad. Intimate relationships rarely appear abusive at the start, and behaviors that start out as attentive and nurturing can shift over time to become emotionally abusive and controlling.

You might have a sense early on that something is not what it appears to be. You can have a feeling or a reaction to something your new partner says or does that doesn't feel right. You can sense something is off, which is what we would call "red flags." Sometimes you get caught up in the novelty or excitement of a new relationship and want to ignore these signs, but pay close attention to your gut feelings. If you notice any red flags, or feel something is not quite right, take a moment to check in with yourself and reference the below warning signs. It is essential to recognize these signs so you can act as soon as possible.

Control

Control is a primary concept in understanding abuse. It may come first in the form of attentiveness, protection, and nurturing. However, in an abusive relationship, these behaviors often become attempt to manage aspects of your life. It is common for an abusive partner to keep track of where you go and where you are, insist on being in constant contact with you, tell you who you can and cannot see, what you should wear, and so on. The abuser may be demanding and angry or may offer more gentle "helpful suggestions." They may embed criticism in their demands, or you may notice over time that there are consequences when you don't take their suggestions.

Name Calling

Name calling, or verbal insults designed to win an argument, demean, or control your feelings of self-worth, can be overt or disguised by joking or playfulness. The intent is always to belittle and devalue the victim. When arguments consistently devolve into assassinating your character and include "always" and "never" statements, they serve no purpose other than to control, undermine, and dominate you. An example is, "You always forget to do what I asked you. Are you just dumb, or is something else wrong with you?"

Yelling

Yelling is commonly known as raising someone's voice, but abusers can use yelling as a form of conditioning. The receiver is conditioned to comply with the yeller, who attempts to impose their will with this behavior. Yelling is a way of wearing down the victim and preventing their expression. Over time, it can whittle away a person's spirit and dignity.

Gaslighting

Gaslighting—a common topic in recent years—is a term taken from a stage play called Gas Light from the 1930s, where a husband plotted his wife's demise by manipulating her into thinking she was crazy. Gaslighting uses psychological manipulation to cause an abuse victim to doubt their perceptions and sense of reality. Gaslighting strategies include instances when the abuser:

- Withholds information.
- Puts their spin on information to fit their agenda.
- Uses jokes and sarcasm to dismiss the victim's feelings and experiences.
- Denies and minimizes a victim's reactions and concerns.
- Acts as though they or the victim did not say what they said or that certain events did not happen.

Common gaslighting phrases may look like the following:

- "I never said that."
- "You never told me that."
- "That never happened."
- "Are you sure you didn't dream that?"

- "You're too sensitive."

Abusers who engage in gaslighting tactics often project things that they have done, such as telling you that you are confused, crazy, or intoxicated if you say what you know to be true or question their version of the facts. In a work environment, the abuser may take credit for your work or ideas and then deny it. They may lie to others about you or take a sliver of truth and blow it up in a way that ruins your reputation. Gaslighters attack you with the information they know to be especially important or sensitive.

Isolation

An abusive person may possibly perceive your spending time with friends and family as a threat and can work to isolate you from them. They may begin this process by criticizing or devaluing your relationships with your friends and family. For example, the abuser may say that your loved ones treat you poorly or take advantage of you, or that time spent with them takes away from your relationship with the abuser.

There may be enough truth in this coercion to influence or confuse you. For instance, you may have confided in your partner about frustrations with a family member, and your partner will remind you of this when you are planning on spending time with that person. Attempts to isolate you are sometimes much more overt. Your abuser may restrict your access to money, transportation, or communication with your friends and family. The loneliness that results from this social isolation can lead to anxiety, depression, increased substance use, and health issues.

Threats

A threat is a statement of intent to cause you damage, pain, or loss. It is an act of coercion from an abuser, with an undercurrent of the potential for violence.

These or similar statements—all reported by victims of abuse—will often target a fear you already have:

- "I will kill myself."
- "I will kill you."
- "If I can't have you, no one will."
- "I will take the kids."
- "I will turn you in to immigration."
- "I will out you to your family."
- "I will ruin your life."
- "I will never let you go."
- "Maybe you just don't want to work here anymore."

Punishment

Punishment is anything your abuser may do in response to any perceived injury, refusal, or rejection. Punishment can come in the form of revenge or conditioning: an abuser seeks revenge to inflict pain, and conditions you to change your behavior. This punishment doesn't have to be just physical either. It can be mental as well. Saying things like "I won't talk to you until you do this for me" can be seen as a form of mental and/or emotional abuse.

Rejecting

Rejecting behavior is any act that refuses to acknowledge your needs and gifts. It can include withholding or declining offers of love, attention, or affection. It is a way of denigrating you and what you have to offer, with the underlying message that you're not wanted or needed.

Neglect

Neglect is a pattern of behaviors used to remove attention and affection and deprive you of your emotional need for belonging, love, and connection. Neglect can include careless behaviors, ignoring, showing interest in other partners, and silent treatment.

Financial Abuse

Financial abuse includes limiting access to funds, withholding financial information, or imposing absolute control of funds—often resembling a parent-to-child dynamic. It is not uncommon in this type of abuse for the victim to have no idea how much their partner makes or to be required to turn over their whole paycheck to the abuser.

WHAT CAUSES SOMEONE TO BECOME AN ABUSER?

The settings we are most exposed to frequently mold our personalities and defining traits. A kind, courteous, and loving personality is more likely to develop in a caring environment where everyone is treated with respect.

On the other hand, a harsh environment where the members' worth is devalued and disregarded is likely to make someone feel uneasy, self-conscious, and afraid. Such a person is more likely to end up developing emotional, verbal, and psychological problems.

1. Childhood may be the source of emotional abuse.

Nobody wakes up one morning and starts acting abusively without understanding what it looks like or what it may accomplish. Parental abuse can include abuse by grandparents, guardians, step-parents, and anyone with authority to make decisions for a child. For example, suppose a grandparent came for a visit and commented to their grandchild about how fat they are or other comments regarding their physical appearance. In that case, it may not seem like abuse because it happens infrequently, and however, derogatory statements still constitute abuse. The grandparent is not trying to help the child gain confidence but is taking it away.

Offhand, hurtful comments and remarks are instances where abuse doesn't necessarily require a pattern from one person. Children can be particularly sensitive to such things, and they can affect them if they occur one too many times, whether or not the person who threw the comment is the child's regular abuser. The more individuals pass a certain remark, the more effect it can have.

Children with weight problems and other similar issues are especially vulnerable. Sometimes, their parents aren't careful enough, and their children can be exposed to hurtful, unconscionable comments from relatives at family gatherings, for instance.

Even worse is when it comes from a parent or step-parent that has a chance to berate and belittle you daily.

Irresponsible Parenting

Setting boundaries and teaching children how to be satisfied, even when they are disappointed that they didn't get what they wanted, are the parents' responsibilities. Constant belittlement can be directed at a wide range of personal traits, from character to behavior to physical appearance.

It is truly sad just how frequently this abusive interaction can occur between parents and their children, but worse yet is how complicated the cause and the goal of such abuse can be. Namely, parents who berate or insult their children with the sole intention of causing harm are very rare and disturbed individuals. Suppose you find yourself under an onslaught of weekly or daily hurtful comments about your behavior, character, or aspects of your appearance that you can change. In that case, you need to consider the underlying cause of your parent's behavior. The chances that your parent hates you are incredibly slim.

In the simplest terms, their hurtful remarks are quite likely the result of sheer incompetence. For instance, if you have some extra weight or develop certain unhealthy habits, your parent's belittling comments might just be their way of expressing that they care about you and are concerned about your health and wellbeing. To be sure, this is a harmful and ineffective approach to parenting, but unfortunately, some parents think that insults and harshness are the only approaches. It is likely that their parents, too, used insults and harsh remarks to make them to change their ways and get on the right track, never teaching them the virtue of support, kind words, and positive reinforcement.

This is where the parent crosses a line between constructive criticism and verbal abuse; the parent can inflict significant emotional damage, so belittlement is still abusive, whether or not the parent is aware of what they're doing. However, this means there is a possibility of talking to your parents about it and explaining how you feel. Even the most ignorant and clueless parents might be able to see the error of their ways if their child explains that the remarks are hurtful and make you feel low and unmotivated. After all, this will show them just how counter-productive their approach is, and they might understand that the way to move forward is to support you and help you, rather than hurl insults at you.

At the very least, understanding that your parents fundamentally wish you well can help you cope with their abusive ways. No child should have to endure verbal attacks, of course, but sometimes, a change in perspective can function as a shield, help you overcome difficulties, and even become motivated. If your parents care about you and want to see you do better, then proving their insults wrong through action should certainly make them regret being hurtful.

This change in perspective can be especially helpful if the abuse you wish to overcome is already a thing of the past. If you suffer because you are unsure if your parents ever loved you due to all the hurtful words they threw at you daily, then understanding their perspective can help you alleviate those doubts. At the end of the day, even if they are abusive and hurtful in their remarks, most parents are just concerned about their children and simply don't know any better.

The best way to identify whether or not your parents insulted you to motivate you is to reflect on how they behave after the object of their criticism has been corrected. If they commend you and the abuse never reoccurs, they most likely want you to do better. On the other hand, truly abusive parents will always find something wrong with you. When you respond and fix what they want, they will invent a new flaw in you, and the cycle will continue all your life. After a certain point, it becomes clear that the fault is not with you.

Learning how to live without being able to control all we wish we could is a necessary part of maturing. A spoilt, arrogant kid thinks they are entitled to everything. As an adult, he or she is unprepared for reality and the sharing of resources and freedoms in light of how they affect other people.

Experiencing Abuse as a Child

A youngster who witnesses their parents verbally abusing one another regularly may be able to accept what they are witnessing as what a "normal" loving relationship looks like. Why would a child assume that abuse is odd or unhealthy if the only relationships they have ever witnessed or experienced contain it?

Being a victim of physical, sexual, or emotional abuse can, unfortunately, happen to people during their formative years (Rowntree, 2007). Research has unequivocally shown that these experiences or being abused as a youngster predisposes the child to continue abusing once they become adults.

Power Being Exalted

Some families have a distinctive culture that exalts violence and power. The main themes in the households where some abusers arise include guns, violence, war, and similar topics. They grow up believing that asserting one's value is accomplished by being physically or emotionally "powerful." In particular, men who grow up in underserved communities oftentimes view dominance over others as a sign of worth and manliness (Violence, 2022).

Neglectful Parents

You may put inadequate self-reliance upon children whose parents were neglectful in raising them. As a result, the infant may develop a strong personality and a will to conquer obstacles. When confronted with and challenged by the needs of his or her partner in a relationship, such a youngster is unwilling to back off. They adopt a "my way or the highway" mentality.

Even if someone learns about abuse as a child, they still have to make decisions as an adult. Every adult can either continue the cycle of abusive behavior or carry it into their relationships, regardless of how they raised them. In reality, many people I know who have experienced emotional abuse have decided not to carry over such practices into new relationships. They successfully prevent emotional abuse from entering their life because they can see the harm it inflicts.

2. Low self-esteem may be the basis of emotional abuse.

A variety of factors can cause people's poor self-esteem. Although few of them involve mistreating others, some do. This is why:

Don't think about yourself

People with poor self-esteem frequently dislike thinking about themselves, and reflection might lead to painfully unfavorable ideas. Finding fault in others and starting disputes are only a couple of the many ways one might stop thinking about themselves. By doing this, one maintains external attention. Therefore, abuse is self-serving, and so is all the volatility it brings.

Compel People to Recognize Their Worth

Bullying tactics are occasionally used by those who feel unloved and unworthy to persuade others of their value. When taken to its utmost, this can turn into emotional abuse in which the offender attempts to coerce the victim into admitting his or her inferiority. It is a method for the individual with low self-esteem to now believe that he or she has value while being incredibly dysfunctional and self-defeating.

Immaturity in General

Some violent people have low emotional IQs, and their age does not accurately reflect their capacity for responsible and rational thought, feeling, and behavior. It's as though the victim is married to a child, except their partner abuses their power by using their adult resources and body.

Abuse cannot be used as a cure-all for poor self-esteem. A failing connection, a lack of intimacy, and avoidance are the only outcomes of such a relationship with others. Because it validates their poor self-esteem, all of them are prescriptions for what isn't desired.

3. A person's genetic makeup might play a role in emotional maltreatment.

Technically, those who suffer from genetic disorders are not abusers. Instead, these are sick people who require medical attention. However, I have added this area to the explanation because some of you might be trying to determine why you are being emotionally abused.

One study examining the mental health characteristics of men who abuse their intimate partners found that abusive men tend to fit into one of three groups. Roughly half were exposed to similar environments during childhood but had no additional genetic, emotional, or personality problems to confound matters. The second group is abusers with Borderline personality traits, who tend to be generally unhappy, uneasy, or unsatisfied. A third group contained anti-social personalities with high levels of dark personality traits (narcissism, psychopathy, Machiavellianism, and sadism).

Interestingly, head injury, particularly damage to the frontal lobe (just behind the forehead, responsible for high-level reasoning) or temporal lobe (the central region of the brain and the emotional, sexual, and anxiety center with functions in regulating attention and impulsivity) can lead to impulsive, aggressive acts (Rowntree, 2007). Even from childhood, head injury and brain damage play a role in behavior and impulse control for a significant proportion of abusers.

Another study found that alcohol and drugs played a significant role in the abuse, with an abusive event 11 times more likely to occur on days when the abuser had been drinking. Anxiety was found in 40% of abusers in one study, with major depression also found to be present in 11%.

The primary psychopathy score concerns empathy for others and a lack of fear and anxiety. It has been robustly associated with reduced neural activity in response to other peoples' emotions, particularly distress. Some scientists argue that primary psychopathy is associated with a lack of anxiety and a lowered fear response due to a genetic predisposition, which is in direct contrast to secondary psychopathy, which is thought to arise from high anxiety and a challenging environment.

Science has shown that our well-being and happiness are largely within our control. While a proportion of our happiness depends on our genetics and past experiences, a big chunk can be changed and tweaked using simple positive psychology exercises.

Diseases of the Mind

Numerous personality problems manifest themselves in incredibly violent and insensitive ways. Narcissistic personality disorder, bipolar disorder (which is truly a mood disease), and borderline personality disorder are a few instances of such disorders. Coexisting with these people frequently entails living in fear when the underlying disorder is not treated.

Impulse Management

Some people struggle to control their desires because of their genetic makeup. They simply don't know how to do this, not because they intend to mistreat their relationships. They frequently overpower and even crush their spouses as a result.

However, there are appropriate therapy and medical treatments to assist individuals in learning to restrict themselves and act more socially. People with genetic predispositions for aggressive and abusive conduct are not purposefully abusive, and taking the appropriate actions to stop bad behavior can assist in holding them responsible. People should avoid having such close ties if they lack the emotional and mental resources to obtain their needed assistance.

4. Substance addiction can make emotional abuse behaviors worse.

Alcohol or drug use alters a person's behavior from what it is when they are sober. Although substance misuse is not the cause of emotional abuse, it might make someone more likely to act in an emotionally abusive manner. When drink or drugs are involved, a person who would ordinarily be polite may display their abusive side. There is no justification for their actions, even though these people might assert that the drugs bring on the abuse.

The user must stop using drugs or alcohol if others have informed them that their intoxication causes abusive behavior. They must be held accountable and rightly classified as abusive if they won't give up their habit, just like anyone who doesn't use drugs would.

EFFECTS OF EMOTIONAL ABUSE

A universal human need is to be understood and to understand. When you are in an abusive relationship, these needs are not met. The victim may have the rational thought that they can learn to understand their partner, which keeps them in the relationship. Victims of this kind of abuse will slowly lose their self-esteem and confidence, usually without knowing it.

When abusers don't understand their partner, it leaves them in this incomprehensible reality where they are faced with the blame for their battering.

Victims of emotional abuse will likely experience:

- Distrust of future relationships.
- They live in the future, "I'll be happy when…"
- Believing that what they do best is actually what they do worst.
- A desire to escape.
- Reluctance to reach conclusions.
- Desire not to be how they are—for example, too sensitive.
- Feeling like time is flying by, but they are missing out on something.
- Fear of being crazy.
- Worried that they aren't as happy as they should be.
- Internalized critical voice.
- A growing sense of self-doubt.

- Loss of self-confidence.
- A want to soul-search and review past experiences with the hope that they can figure out what happened.
- Worried that something is wrong with them.
- Uncertain as to how they come across.
- Constantly on guard.
- Loss of enthusiasm.
- Distrust of their spontaneity.

Emotional abuse kills the spirit and removes life's joy. It changes the victim's reality because their abuser responds in a way that is odd for what is happening. The victim believes the abuser to be telling them the truth and can come up with a million reasons for what he says.

The victim is stuck living on hope. They cling to the moments when things seem normal and believe the upsets will slowly disappear. Many victims have said that their partners occasionally bought them things, complimented their looks, and shared something personal. From time to time, their expectations would grow, and they would forget what their abuser had done. They would hope for a better future, and this hope kept them in the relationship.

We are going to take a look at an interaction that shows the discrepancy in the communication that leaves the partner confused:

Amy and James had three children, two of whom were in college. On the outside, their marriage looked great, but James had become more abusive over the years. Amy shared this story about their relationship.

James called the house and asked to speak with their daughter. Amy told him she was taking a shower and asked if he wanted her to call him back.

He replied, "Yes," and said, "she called me asking about the stereo. Let her know that I don't know what's wrong."

"Okay," Amy said, "I'll let her know."

He replied, "No, I can call back later, or she can call when she gets the chance."

"Okay," Amy said, "what message would you like me to give her?"

James returned full of rage, "I didn't ask you to write down a message!"

Amy was in pain and shock at his outburst. Additionally, she was trying to comprehend his reasoning for believing that he had asked her to deliver a message. Everybody in their household would write down messages for each other. She had so many emotions going through her head that she could barely speak. She ended the call with, "I'll let her know you called. Bye."

Amy spent the rest of the day thinking, "If I hadn't asked him about his message, I wouldn't feel this way." She kept thinking she said something wrong, and she now felt like a failure. She had been thinking about returning to work, but now she was wondering if she could do it since she couldn't even relate to her husband.

James never did things like this when there were other people around. While Amy tried to talk with her husband about the problems, he always reverted to diverting, accusing, discounting, or denying.

Emotional abuse leaves the victim confused and frustrated and can lead to depression and anxiety. One theory even suggests that emotional abuse could contribute to developing chronic fatigue syndrome and fibromyalgia. Though hard to see, emotional abuse leaves indelible marks on its victims.

2

UNRAVELING ALL THE TACTICS

"Don't ask me why I didn't leave, he made my world so small, I couldn't see the exit. I'm surprised I got out at all."

— RUPI KAUR

Once you have gotten accustomed to spotting the traits and characteristics of the emotionally abusive person, it will become easy to spot them. You will also start to notice that you feel drained after spending time with them. This chapter will help teach you about the different traits, characteristics, and types of emotional abuse.

You can find psychological abuse everywhere. These abusers are out there, and it's very hard to avoid them. But it is possible to identify them from the way they act. This is the reason why it is so important to be on the alert and to understand how to interpret what could be their actual intentions. These abusive people are also known as toxic people. They are draining, hard to deal with, and leave you feeling used (Young, 2017).

In the majority of cases, they create damage by using the power they have over others through covert abuse. This may seem weird, but this abuse is frequently concealed, which is why there is a difference between real-time recognition and retrospective recognition.

COVERT AND OVERT EMOTIONAL ABUSE

When they hear the word "abuse," many individuals think of domestic violence-related behaviors like shoving, yelling, name-calling, striking, spitting, or obstructing people's paths. Usually, it is simple to identify these overt actions (Violence, 2022). However, overt abuse like this, which is obvious to see and obviously wrong, is not the only form of deception abusers may employ on their victims.

The word "covert" means "hidden" or "secret," and because the symptoms of covert emotional abuse are so challenging to identify and characterize, it is almost impossible to confront them. This harmful form of abuse can increase in all kinds of relationships, and when it does, the victim's body, mind, and soul are all but destroyed.

There are many different types of covert emotional abuse, including deceptive tactics like lying and concealing information. Few people possess the emotional intelligence necessary to recognize and react to covert emotional abuse when it is occurring since it is difficult to identify by nature. We will provide tips to help one recognize when this is going on since this ambiguity occasionally exists amongst the least likely of suspects (pastors, counselors, and friends).

A relationship might end with just one emotionally abusive act that is committed repeatedly. If done regularly, lying frequently, acting like the victim, or dismissing the other person's worries will destroy the safety and trust that should exist between people who are deeply connected. However, when some or all emotionally abusive behaviors occur simultaneously, it puts the victim in a permanent state of anxious bewilderment.

The victim of stressful perplexity begins to mistrust and question everything, even their own observations and experiences. If left unresolved and untreated, post-traumatic stress disorder eventually results from ongoing stressful disorientation.

A victim of ongoing emotional abuse has neither an internal nor an external safe area. Their immunological system is severely strained resulting in consequent bodily effects and symptoms. When their abuser is spoken to or seen, some victims, for instance, may have such pronounced increases or decreases in blood pressure that they may pass out or have a heart attack. Studies have shown that heart attack risk is increased by emotional trauma, such as physical abuse, or the death of a spouse, mental or post-traumatic stress disorder.

In a British study released in the Journal of the American Heart Association, aimed to close knowledge gaps about the connection between domestic violence and cardiovascular disease, the world's leading cause of death for women. In the United States, one in four women had gone through domestic abuse that was so severe that it left them injured, in need of medical attention, or showing signs of post-traumatic stress disorder (Domestic Abuse May Do Long-Term Damage to Women's Health, 2022).

In a study in the Journal of the American Heart Association, children who faced severe adversity such as verbal, physical, or emotional abuse or who lived with drug or alcohol addicts had a 50% higher risk of developing cardiovascular disease as adults than those who had less exposure to trauma. By middle age, those with mild exposure had a 60% higher risk of dying from any cause (Traumatic Childhood Increases Lifelong Risk for Heart Disease, Early Death, 2022).

According to researchers, this may be the case because individuals who experience significant adversity as youngsters have a range of behavioral and biochemical reactions that are still poorly understood (Guillen, 2022). People are more prone to adopt unhealthy coping techniques, including smoking and bad eating habits, which increase the likelihood of developing conventional cardiovascular risk factors, such as high blood pressure, inflammation, diabetes, and obesity.

However, the repercussions of covert emotional abuse are rarely concealed. This is a damaging sort of abuse, and because it is typically concealed, it is all the more hurtful and challenging to define and notice.

You can tell if you are being emotionally abused, though. Do they avoid accepting responsibility for their conduct at all costs? That is the most telling red flag. It is possible that this individual never expresses regret for wrongdoing or that, when they do, it is in a way that deflects blame from themselves.

When you try to confront an abuser, they may sidestep you by changing the subject, leading you into a rabbit hole, or abruptly stating that they must go due to a "prior commitment." You would be right to assume that you are experiencing emotional abuse if the offending party consistently finds a means to escape accountability for their deeds. Alternately, it is abuse if they repeatedly apologize yet carry on with their damaging behavior habits.

Although it can happen in other settings, such as families, schools, and workplaces, covert emotional abuse frequently occurs in romantic relationships.

For example, an abusive coworker may begin purposefully excluding a colleague from email threads to make him or her appear unprepared, unaware, and illiterate.

Similarly, a school bully may invite everyone to a birthday celebration but leave out one student. When confronted by that person, the bully would respond, "Well, you just must not have gotten it in the mail."

Have you noticed that this response has some plausibility and cannot be refuted? These less serious incidents could start stressful uncertainty that causes the victim to doubt their own experiences. Gaslighting is the term for this.

Having damaged sentiments is not the goal of covert emotional abuse. It is the medical term used to describe the psychological and bodily harm that results from repeatedly manipulating a victim.

We must start comprehending, avoiding, and responding to emotional abuse better because it has long-lasting physical effects. Some countries, such as the UK for example, have gone so far as to pass legislation which outlaws various types of psychological and emotional abuse

Therefore, it is the counselor's, HR department's, school administrator's, or first point of contact's job to take these complaints seriously and look into them when someone believes they have been subjected to emotional abuse. They must remember that although this kind of abuse is difficult to detect, the pain and stress are genuine and legitimate.

We must pay attention to and respect victims since nothing is always as it seems. It's not impossible to end covert emotional abuse just because it is hard to spot. It can and ought to.

SYMPTOMS OF COVERT ABUSE AND GETTING ASSISTANCE

The indications of covert abuse are numerous and diverse. The main distinction between covert and overt abuse is how it is carried out. Because of this, covert domestic violence frequently exhibits some traits in common with overt abuse (Violence, 2022).

Domestic abusers frequently keep their victims by themselves to conceal and continue their abuse. Extreme isolation cases include transferring a family to a new town or city without any close friends, family members, or allies. Or they could be less obvious, subtly hinting that the person's friends and family don't genuinely want to be around them.

Gaslighting is a common tactic used by covert abusers to keep their victims silent, submissive, and trapped. As mentioned earlier, gaslighting involves disturbing the subject to make them doubt their perception of reality. Because it undermines the victim's sense of legitimacy and self-worth, this is the ideal tactic for covert domestic violence.

Continual abuse. Contrary to popular belief, covert abuse is rarely a single incident but causes prolonged victim suffering regularly. To maintain their control, domestic violence abusers frequently choose partners, friends, or other people close to them who will not speak out against abuse. The instability of the victim is a key component of covert abuse.

Guilt and low self-esteem in the victim of the assault. People who have undergone covert abuse, domestic violence, or domestic abuse may feel shame, remorse, uncertainty, and disgust toward themselves since it tries to keep the individual on edge and maintain the upper hand (Higgins, 2016). They can believe that they are to blame for the abuse, that they are flawed or unlovable, or that the person who had always been sensitive and kind has suddenly turned cruel.

The implied threat of violence. Not all domestic abuse results in overt conflict. Instead, emotional or mental abuse, which harms a person's sense of security, sense of self, and sense of normalcy, can be inflicted during domestic abuse just as easily. Another person's physical, mental, or emotional well-being is harmed through covert abuse, making it violent.

Getting Assistance After Abuse

Many services are accessible to persons who have been abused, including those who have been assaulted covertly. Even though covert abuse may be challenging to overcome—partly due to its clandestine, well-hidden character. People who have encountered any kind of abuse are frequently advised to join support groups since victims of abuse frequently feel alone and alienated from their peers. People who have experienced abuse may find comfort in joining support groups, and they might also aid in identifying abusive patterns and conduct that was once seen as normal.

Getting help frequently entails leaving the abuser. This is not always possible because families often need to stay together, and jobs cannot always be left behind. However, finding safety is of the highest importance; thus, escaping abuse typically involves looking for financial, legal, or law enforcement support. You can lessen the hardship of leaving an abusive relationship by speaking with local law enforcement officials, consulting a lawyer, and applying for state and federal financial aid programs.

THE NARCISSISTIC PERSONALITY DISORDER (NPD)

If you already know your partner has a narcissistic personality, you're somewhat of an expert on how difficult a relationship with them can be. Maybe you know what they are about, or perhaps you see who they are and what they are doing to you, but you aren't sure how to let go. Or you have managed to walk away, but you are worried you'll either go back or that you'll never find anyone better. These are all valid concerns, which is why we are starting at square one with getting your life back.

The term *narcissism* is used so often that its true meaning gets confused. It's most commonly related to people with strong personalities and confidence borders on arrogance. Those individuals need to dominate the conversation even if the topics aren't their strongest areas, and their egos influence their need to be the center of attention. Although many of these behaviors sound similar to a narcissist's personality, there are important differences that set them apart.

NPD is a mental condition that affects approximately one percent of the population, higher in men than women. Extreme arrogance, a lack of empathy, and deep admiration characterize this state of mind. The most distinguishing characteristic of the narcissistic personality is its sense of superiority. Narcissists are concerned about wealth, reputation, and pride and believe that special treatment is warranted for their "station."

Someone with narcissistic personality disorder should not be mistaken for someone with a high sense of self-worth. People with high self-esteem can be modest, whereas narcissists, who usually have low self-esteem, cannot. They are arrogant and presumptuous, and they are deafeningly insensitive to the feelings and needs of others. The condition also hurts a person's quality of life and other symptoms.

Overall, the person may be dissatisfied with their life and frustrated when others do not admire them or do not treat them differently than they would like to be treated. All important areas of one's life are affected; work, personal, social, and incredibly, the individual is unaware that their actions harm their interpersonal relationships. People do not feel comfortable around narcissistic people, and narcissists are dissatisfied with their jobs, social lives, and other aspects of their lives.

A narcissistic personality disorder is characterized by individuals who, on the surface, appear to be upbeat and friendly. They are also supposedly cheerful, nice, and desirable gaslighters. Indeed, the "narcissistic perverts," as they are sometimes referred to (with no sexual connotation in mind), are people who suffer from a terrible lack of self-confidence, most of the time without being aware of it, and who present themselves with a completely different appearance.

As a result, these narcissists often believe that they are superior to the public, must be respected and idolized, and should not be criticized. Several factors contribute to narcissistic personality disorder. Like all psychological disorders, the exact cause of narcissistic personality disorder is unknown. However, researchers believe that it begins in childhood.

Certain circumstances, such as the inability to comprehend and integrate the feeling of empathy, can act as triggers. For example, narcissism can be a defense mechanism against abuse and traumatic experiences or a way to meet up to the high expectations of your parents.

There is much debate about the many causes of Narcissism. One school of thought considers Narcissism a social failing, particularly due to parental upbringing. Parents who don't set a good example for their children may actually be the root cause for their children becoming narcissistic as well.

Some experts have suggested a neurobiological or genetic disorder, but no evidence has been presented to support this theory. The dust is far from settled, and the nature-nurture debate rumbles on.

The Role of Narcissism in Covert Abuse

Domestic violence committed by a covert narcissist, or a narcissist whose problem presents in a quieter, less outspoken manner than the average individual with narcissistic personality disorder, is one example of covert abuse (NPD). Although NPD is not a need for abuse, it may play a role in covert abuse because narcissists have mastered the art of hiding their disturbing thoughts and conduct from the public to preserve their reputation and standing. Because a narcissist may be more concerned with how they are perceived or thought of by others than a member of the general public, covert abuse may go hand in hand with covert narcissism or, in fact, overt narcissism.

MANIPULATION AND GUILT TRIPPING

A guilt trip consists of making another person feel guilty or fully accountable for changing their behavior or carrying out a particular action. People can use guilt as a tool to influence the thoughts, feelings, and actions of others since guilt has the potential to be a strong motivator of human conduct.

Sometimes this may entail relying on something for which a person already feels guilty. In other situations, people may create unwarranted guilt or responsibility to control the other person's sentiments and actions.

You've experienced guilt trips if someone has made you feel awful about something you did (or didn't do) and then used those negative emotions to persuade you to do something for them.

VARIOUS GUILT TRIPS

Many different kinds of guilt can appear in a relationship, but they are all intended to make the other person feel humiliated and give in to their demands.

Think about the following examples of manipulation through guilt:

Moral Guilt

Let's imagine your husband prefers you to stay at home and disagrees with your desire to spend the weekend gambling at a casino with buddies.

To try to make you feel bad and cancel the outing, they might lecture you about how clubbing at a young age is not "right." Moral shame sets in when someone tries to persuade you that their choice or method is better and yours is evil.

Sympathy-Seeking

Another way guilt trippers may make someone feel bad is by acting as if they have been hurt. In trying to make the other person feel bad and change their behavior out of empathy for their transgression, the guilt tripper will go on and on about how the other person's behavior has harmed them (Higgins, 2016).

Manipulation

When one person plans to make the other person feel guilty so they will feel compelled to do something they would not normally do, this is called simple manipulation and can occur in relationships. This enables the guilt tripper to guarantee their success.

Conflict Avoidance

This type of guilt-tripping may manifest as the guilty tripper displaying outward signs of distress while adamantly maintaining that everything is fine. The hope is that the other person will sense the guilt tripper's feelings, feel awful, and behave differently. In some instances, people could use guilt trips to avoid addressing a problem head-on. It enables people to achieve their goals without directly confronting one another or giving the cold shoulder, forcing the person to change.

Gaslighting

Relationships are hard work. Everyone knows this. However, everyone fails to realize that relationships can be more complex when stuck with a deliberate liar. And when it comes to bad relationship partners, there is none as terrible as the gaslighter.

The term "gaslighting" refers to an abusive activity in which victims are made to doubt themselves and their real-life decisions. They are confused and believe they are going insane by a fraudulent activity established by the abuser.

As a result of this mental manipulation, the gaslighter, or the person who performs it, leads the victim to believe they are living in a reality that differs from objective reality, causing them to feel wrong. This undermines their sense of security and certainty, thereby committing what is known as "true brainwashing."

According to research carried out by relevant psychology organizations, the vast majority of gaslighting victims and perpetrators are relatively close, usually associates or close relatives of the victim (Guillen, 2022). Gaslighting is comparable to behavioral torture techniques performed during the cold war era. It is a harsh psychological coercion tactic in which the perpetrator repeatedly questions the validity of their victim's ideas until the victim is utterly oblivious of their reality in order to achieve complete control over them.

Many psychologists consider gaslighting to be a serious psychological assault that instills suspicions in the other's mind. It can be extremely confusing and victims will start questioning their own thoughts and assumptions when being gaslit.

Some even consider it to be a form of genuine brainwashing. Even though it looks to be a complicated approach to adopt, it is more common than one might imagine, particularly in partnerships or intimate family relationships. Gaslighting is a form of extreme psychological abuse, and it is synonymous with emotional abuse for many, and for a good reason.

Gaslighters have a variety of tricks to torture their victims. The abuser could intentionally provide incorrect information to their victims to be more confused about their identity and ignorant of their situation. The abuser's purpose is to cause their victims to doubt their own thoughts and recall of a particular situation.

Psychopaths typically perpetrate gaslighting with a personality disorder characterized by a lack of empathy toward others and increased antisocial conduct and activity.

People with such personality features can abuse others without feeling guilty or humiliated because they do not have these characteristics. Regular people who gaslight will most likely be unconvincing because it will reveal in their body language and facial expressions (Higgins, 2016). Despite this, they may be incredibly convincing liars and manipulators, much like psychopaths. Their goal is to cause their target's notion of truth to be undermined by making the lies appear genuine.

Lying

One of the most common ways and strategies used by abusers to exert authority and control over their victims is lying.

Lying is a form of abuse and it clouds the victim's perception of reality and makes it easier for the liar to escape responsibility for the incident by frequently placing the blame on the victim. Lies can be used as a hidden form of abuse by coworkers, significant others, friends, or family.

Additionally, lying opens the door for physical abuse and other forms of maltreatment. Although everyone makes mistakes, even small lies can easily lead to outright manipulation of a person or circumstance.

Stressful bewilderment is a key component of covert abuse since it is the feeling that abusers want their victims to have when they lie to them.

Lying is a subtle form of abuse that makes the sufferer more anxious and makes them less able to think clearly. A bewildered victim is less likely to act swiftly, trust their instincts, and confront the liar. An abuser can lie in many different ways to control their victim.

Understanding the types and risks of lying is essential to prevent stressful confusion. They include:

Black Lies: These are outright lies that an abuser tells to get what they want at the expense of the victim they are deceiving. Consider a real estate agent who inflates the price of a home by lying about the state of the subsurface plumbing to increase their commission. In other words, out of self-interest, the realtor takes advantage of the buyer's ignorance of current affairs. Abusers also frequently use the lie, "I deposited the check."

However, the abuser has more financial control over the victim if you deposit that check into his or her personal account rather than the joint one. If the check was never deposited, the attacker obtains control over the victim's perplexity and worry when they start to question where the money went or if it ever existed at all. You can find some of these lies with closer examination. To establish control over the victim or obtain power, wealth, position, or other advantages, abusers employ these lies as their main tactic.

White Lies: Everyone is aware of this kind of fraud, which is regrettably typical. White falsehoods are difficult to debunk because they are minute, seemingly dismissing barriers to reality. They are occasionally employed for legitimate reasons, such as when a friend asks you if you like her new hairstyle. You don't actually like it, but you tell her you do to spare her feelings.

White falsehoods have more influence over others because they are harder to track down. Their most pernicious application is when the abuser tells others white lies about the victim because those lies gradually encourage others to perceive the victim differently. For instance, an abuser may reassure friends and family that "everything is wonderful" during a particularly trying time. We're just fine.

However, others close to the relationship perceive the victim's behavior as unpredictable, erratic, and occasionally unstable. This strategy effectively separates the victim from others over time. Even though each lie may initially be too minor to be noticed or addressed, with time and repetition, it will become apparent to others, changing how they perceive the person.

Half-Truths: Half-truths are explanations of what occurred that enable the abuser to absolve themselves of guilt. The liar's strategy is to tell just enough of the truth to appear credible. For instance, saying, "He roared at me," without mentioning the circumstances that led to the argument. This suppression of crucial information creates an impression that is more favorable to the abuser.

Broken Promises: When questioned, abusers find it difficult to accept this type of lying; they will try to excuse themselves. A liar is someone who makes a commitment to attend your office party but then backs out at the last minute. They will attempt to justify their behavior by stating that they had a difficult day or didn't believe you wanted them to go. Broken promises can make the sufferer appear dishonest in front of others, much like a white lie. Always remember that a broken promise is the same as a lie.

Forgetting: Claiming to have forgotten a duty or commitment—for example, "Oh, I forgot you wanted me home early tonight"—is manipulation, similar to breaking commitments. It may persuade the victim that the abuser merely made an error. Never discount persistent "forgetfulness."

Denial: To avoid being discovered or accepting blame, liars will say or do anything, including outright denying the truth, no matter how clear it may seem. When presented with facts and evidence, if someone contests their veracity, they are probably lying.

Remember, emotionally stable individuals do not often tell lies. Transparency is desirable because it brings individuals together, particularly in interactions with close family and friends. Constant lying separates individuals and prohibits genuine relationships; a truly caring lover, parent, sibling, friend, etc., will not do so. It is important to keep track of and address any combination and frequency of these kinds of lies.

Isolation

When someone is holding someone inside and forbidding them from leaving, they engage in isolation as a form of abuse. This can be done in various ways, whether it is controlling what they wear or not letting them have any form of freedom. This can also happen when somebody makes someone feel worthless and that they are a burden to society.

This form of abuse can cause a person to become so withdrawn that they stop trying in life because they don't care anymore. It can also cause that person to become suicidal because of their isolation from the outside world. This is a very hard thing for anybody to handle, but because so many people have been through it and survived, it gives strength to those who are being abused and helps them to believe that they will be okay.

Catastrophizing

Catastrophizing is an emotional abuse tactic where the abuser tries to convince the victim that the consequences of not doing what they are told to do are dire, imaginary, and imminent. Catastrophizing can take a form as benign as "I'll never see my children again" to "You are going to get us killed." Used frequently enough, it can create an atmosphere of fear in which many victims live.

"I'm leaving you" threats are a form of emotional abuse. The abuser threatens to leave the victim if they don't do or give whatever it is the abuser wants. This can take on a very manipulative form because it makes it seem as though the abuser is only leaving because they want to protect their partner from something very bad that is about to happen, not because they feel entitled to something.

Catastrophizing is a sneaky habit that one can use to hurt other people. Catastrophizing is when someone exaggerates a situation or imagines the worst-case scenario to make another person fearful and codependent in a bad way. This strategy may be used by the person who harms others by catastrophizing to defend their own furious or outrageous reactions to situations. Catastrophizing is frequently used to misplace the abuser in the victim role. One may also use it to instill fear or uncertainty in the victim's psyche to keep them immobile and reliant on the relationship.

An abuser may use catastrophizing to undermine their partner's sense of security and distort how they see events, in addition to frightening victims into staying with them. Because it robs the victim of their individuality, that form of connection is much more crippling than others.

Giving The Silent Treatment

An unwillingness to verbally interact with another person is known as the silent treatment. Even refusing to acknowledge the other person's presence can be used as the silent treatment.

Abusers often give their partners the silent treatment. They will with-hold everything they need, denying affection, and completely ignoring them when they are around. This silence is done to hurt their partner as a form of emotional abuse or passive-aggressive behavior.

It is time for abusers to end this silent treatment. It is a form of emotional abuse and a form of passive-aggressive behavior that can anger a partner and makes them feel as if they've been abandoned. Your partner may have endured months, even years, of the silent treatment, so you may want to end it now before it damages your relationship beyond repair.

As long as the abuser uses the silent treatment, they aren't really listening to what their partner has to say and are making decisions for them. There are several reasons why people utilize silent treatment. These consist of:

- **Avoidance:** Sometimes, during a conversation, people remain silent because they are at a loss for words or wish to avoid conflict.

- **Communication:** If a person does not know how to express their thoughts but wants their spouse to know they are upset, they may give them the silent treatment.
- **Punishment:** Silence as a method of punishment, control, or dominance over another person is emotional abuse.

This behavior isn't viewed as "normal" or "acceptable," but it becomes the norm because most people don't see it as a negative behavior.

Several warning signs indicate that your partner might be utilizing the silent treatment as a form of abusive behavior. If you suspect your partner is giving you the silent treatment, you may want to end this and address the issues that are causing it in the first place.

Outright Insults, Name-Calling, and Verbal Abuse

One of the most destructive and heartbreaking forms of abuse is when someone constantly insults, belittles, and puts down the victim. This type of abuse is called "outright insult" or "name-calling." It's one of the most common types of emotional abuse in relationships today.

Sometimes people call each other jerk, idiot, etc., but name-calling becomes verbal abuse when it is used to undercut a person's self-esteem and dignity or make them feel bad about themselves. How name-calling makes you feel:

- Name-calling brings up feelings of anxiety and insecurity.
- The attitude behind it makes the victim feel inferior and inadequate.
- It also hampers a person's self-esteem, as others constantly make fun of or downgrade them, thus creating low self-confidence.

The name-caller may be trying to hurt the victim emotionally or make them feel inferior to try and get more of their time and attention. Name-calling affects you on many different levels:

- It takes apart your self-esteem.

- It makes you feel unloved, unwanted, and unimportant.
- It feels degrading as it is directed at you/another person as a means of punishment or control.
- It usually comes from an insecure person trying to exert power over someone else.
- It can be an attempt to make the victim feel bad about themselves so that they will stay in a relationship.

Therefore, name-calling is a form of emotional abuse, and it can be particularly damaging to children and young people, as it hampers their self-esteem and weakens their confidence.

Playing the Victim

Do you know anyone seeking revenge by taking on a disempowering victim identity? They may proclaim to be the victim of a spouse, child, or boss; in reality, they are inflicting emotional abuse on themselves or others.

Playing the victim helps them feel better about themselves and maintain control over situations that feel out of their control at the time. It also helps them avoid personal responsibility for their actions. Emotional abusers do the following:

- They take on the role of victim to get attention, get forgiveness, or gain sympathy.
- They may blame others, especially their spouse and children, to make themselves more acceptable.
- They may not recognize that they are being abusive by joining in on the abuse they dish out to others and even themselves.
- They do not believe they are entitled to receive respect or love from anyone.
- They do not believe that they have any real control over anything.
- They are too proud or narcissistic to admit that they are wrong.
- They are unaware of the effects of their behavior on others.

But why do the abusers take on a victim identity? This is because:

- Something happened in their past that created lasting feelings of shame and blame.
- They grew up in an environment where an adult abused them and now project that abuse onto others.
- They were not given respect or love as a child, so they don't know how to give it to others—and they don't understand why others would want it from them.
- They may believe that they are entitled to bully others, and they may be projecting their victimhood by playing the victim role for themselves.

Playing the victim is a form of emotional abuse used to control others and make them feel bad about themselves. It's an attempt to manipulate, degrade, and exploit others.

Love-Bombing

Love-bombing is a behavior in which one showers another person with romantic and/or sexual attention, such as gifts, compliments, and promises of commitment.

While love-bombing can be just what the other person needs to boost morale and retain the relationship for a little while longer, it is also often used as a manipulative tool. Love bombs are typically used by people who control their victim's emotions to maximize compliance with requirements or expectations from an abuser.

The victim of a love-bombing relationship is often expected to be the primary focus and sole source of attention. The love-bomber rarely acknowledges or even hears about the accomplishments or needs of others in their life.

An emotional abuser uses false compliments, such as "you are beautiful," "you are smart," or "everything is great," when they want something from their victim. One can use this sense of false validation to control or force the target to stay in an abusive relationship.

It isolates their partner by making them feel like they are the most special and perfect person in the world. Love-bombing is a subtle way of intimidating others into doing what the abuser wants.

EMOTIONAL ABUSE WORKSHEET

This form was created to help you identify the different ways emotional abuse may occur in your relationship, and to help you take steps toward changing the pattern. The form is not meant to take the place of counseling or professional advice.

If you need immediate help, please contact a counselor or other support resource.

Which of these tactics have you suffered from in the past?

- Isolation
- The Silent Treatment
- Gaslighting
- Love-Bombing
- Playing the Victim
- Outright Insults

....

....

....

Describe a scenario where you suffered the abusive tactics you wrote down.

....

....

....

In your own words, describe the main problem you are facing and the negative behavior of your partner. Include examples.

....

....

....

Write down anything that you have said or done to contribute to this problem.

....

....

....

What do you think motivates your partner to behave in this way? For example, what were their parents like? What about their relationships with other people growing up? What about their past experiences?

....

....

....

Write down your thoughts about when the abuse began. Can you see any pattern? What was going on?

....

....

....

Who are the most important people in your life?

....

....

....

Who can you talk to them about this situation? List at least three people. If you need help right away, contact one of them.

....

....

....

Write down anything you can do to escape the situation.

....

....

....

3

GETTING READY TO SURMOUNT THE CHALLENGES

Are you ready to tackle a new challenge? If you or someone close to you has suffered from traumatic emotional abuse, then it is important to understand that there is hope. Recovery isn't easy and it doesn't happen overnight, but with the right self-help tools, emotional distance from the trauma, and some therapeutic support, you can heal.

WILL AN ABUSER JUST LET YOU LEAVE?

When they learn that someone is in an unhealthy or abusive relationship, many people's first thought is, "Why don't they leave?" This reaction may seem natural if you've never been in an abusive relationship and just put the deuces up and go about your business, right? But here's the thing: it's never as simple as "just leaving" when it comes to relationship violence.

Leaving an abusive relationship is difficult for a variety of reasons. There are several possibilities for why someone in an unhealthy or toxic relationship could stay with their partner.

- **Because society normalizes destructive behavior, people may fail to recognize that their relationship is abusive.** When you believe that harmful or abusive actions are typical, it is difficult to recognize your relationship as abusive, and there's no reason to seek treatment.
- **Emotional abuse erodes your self-esteem, making it appear impossible to begin again.** Because no violence is involved, people in emotionally abusive relationships may not realize they are being mistreated. Furthermore, many people disregard or minimize emotional abuse because they believe it is not as severe as physical abuse. It's hard for those in abusive relationships to leave their spouses after being made to feel worthless and as if there's no other alternative for them.
- **The abuse cycle.** A honeymoon phase of reconciliation follows every instance of abuse. When an abusive situation occurs, the abuser frequently does something pleasant or apologizes and promises they will never do it again. This causes their partner to downplay actual abusive behavior.
- **Leaving is risky.** Leaving an abusive relationship is often not just emotionally challenging but physically dangerous. The most difficult moment in an abusive relationship is immediately following the breakup. Compared to any other relationship period, women are 70 times more likely to die in the weeks after leaving an abusive partner (Forray, & Yonkers, K. 2021).

People in abusive relationships frequently make multiple attempts to break up with their partner before the split-up stays. A person in an abusive relationship will typically attempt to leave seven times before finally leaving for good! Yes, you heard me right, seven times. Victims will typically leave, return to their abusers, then attempt to leave again. It is a terribly destructive loop to get caught up in.

- **Society fosters a "ride-or-die" mentality.** Those in toxic or violent relationships may stay with their partner or rekindle their relationship after a breakup because they are pressured not to give up, forgive and forget, or "ride it out." Pop culture romanticizes being a "ride-or-die" for your pals and romantic partners, portraying people as wrong for leaving (Young, 2017). And while loyalty is admirable, a real friend or partner would never put you in danger or do you harm. Continuing to stay with an abusive and manipulative partner is never the right decision!

- **They believe they are personally responsible for their partner's behavior.** Following a quarrel, an abuser will turn the situation around and make their spouse feel guilty or at fault. Gaslighting is a term used to describe this type of behavior.

- **They feel that if they persevere, things will improve.** As a result of their love for their partners and the hope that things will change, many people in violent relationships continue. They may also assume their partner's behavior results from difficult circumstances or believe they can alter their relationship if they are a better partner. Never stay in a relationship when you expect the other person to change their behavior for the better.

- **There is peer pressure to be in the perfect relationship.** There is tremendous pressure to be in the perfect relationship, and some societies and social media add to this strain.

- **Concern about how others will react.** People in abusive relationships frequently feel ashamed to disclose that their partner is abusive for fear of being judged, blamed, marginalized, pitied, or looked down on. For example, in some LGBTQIA* relationships, someone may stay with their partner out of fear of being outed. There are also a few societies where divorces are still a stigma; such as Islam, Catholicism, Judaism, Hinduism, and Christianity.

- **They share a life.** Marriage, children, and shared finances are frequently significant reasons people remain in violent relationships. This dependence is heightened in relationships where one partner has a different ability than the other. However, similar characteristics, such as shared social groups and living arrangements, influence young people's decisions to continue in partnerships.

How To Leave an Abusive Relationship

There are many reasons an individual wants to leave an abusive relationship. Yes, this means you! You deserve and need a safe and healthy life, where you are not constantly being objectified and belittled. The only way to escape this is by leaving your abuser and finding the confidence to know that there is more than one way to go about things.

Step 1: Emotionally prepare yourself.

It is challenging to generate the bravery to leave if you've been regularly subjected to words and actions that make you feel worthless and you are too beaten down to trust yourself.

Step 2: Lay the foundation.

You must begin arranging your exit, which includes determining all logistical and legal requirements so that you (and your children) can leave securely. Meanwhile, consider the following expert advice:

Step 3: Get out as soon as possible.

Choose a safe time, not the best moment. There is no proper time to leave, so it comes down to finding a safe time, which usually means when you're at home and your partner is either at work, out with friends, or visiting relatives.

Step 4: After you've left the house:

Keep your whereabouts hidden.

Avoid contact with your abuser and his or her support system. You will be at risk of further abuse if they know where you are. Remember, your identity and location are confidential unless you provide specific permission.

Submit a restraining order.

Alternatively, have your lawyer do it right now. A piece of paper can help keep your partner away from you and your children. If you phone the police and say, "This individual is here, and I have a restraining order," it puts you at the top of the list. They rush out when the police realize it's in the system.

Stop communicating with your partner.

If the abuser does not hear from you, it is much less likely that they will continue to abuse you. They'll stay for a specific time before moving on to their next victim and start hunting for the next person they can manipulate.

Don't leave any hints.

Don't forward any bills or change your address on your driver's license. You can't do any of these things since they make it easier for someone to find you. Having a cell phone number and a utility bill forwarded is generally enough to help an abuser track down the person they are looking for.

Prepare to dial 911.

If your abuser shows up where you are, shows up at work, or sees you on the street, you must phone 911 immediately and say, "I have a restraining order. This person is close to me. I require immediate assistance."

When you are in a violent relationship, your first concern should be to get yourself and your children to safety. According to statistics, the most hazardous time for women living with batterers is when they leave the relationship (Hing, O'Mullan, Mainey, Nuske, Breen, & Taylor, 2021). While most battered wives and partners are women, all this advice applies equally to battered men.

This means you'll need to live somewhere the abuser can't find you, such as a battered women's shelter, a hotel, or the house of a friend the abuser doesn't know. Don't go to your parents' house, your closest friend's house, or any other location where the abuser might seek you.

WHY LEAVING MAY BE DIFFICULT

Unfortunately, the most dangerous period in an abusive relationship is when the victim attempts to escape; this is when the abuser is likely to kill him or her. Homicide is one of the top 10 causes of mortality for women ages 20 to 44 in the US, and partners kill more women than anybody else (Focht, 2013).

The threat to one's safety isn't the only reason many people struggle to exit an abusive relationship. Nobody wants to be mistreated, yet people may blame themselves or grow up believing that abuse is a typical aspect of being in a close relationship (Rodgers, 2022). If getting out of a situation was as simple as people believe, everyone would leave at the first indication of trouble.

Difficulties Leaving an Abusive Partner

The ending of an abusive relationship is not guaranteed or automatic; it may never happen. Survivors sometimes have trouble ending their relationships even when they have the opportunity to do so.

Shame/Social Acceptance

Many people believe that domestic violence is acceptable. When faced with queries from friends and family, such as "What did you do to cause him to hit you," comments like, "You must not have minded him treating you that way because you stayed so long," can deter some people from leaving. The longer a person stays, the more shame they feel for being in an abusive relationship and then for not terminating it promptly. This shame might make leaving the relationship much more difficult.

Money

Ending a relationship, particularly a marriage, can be highly costly, and finding a safe location to reside in can cost hundreds or thousands of dollars. Many people do not earn enough money to maintain themselves without a spouse's income, so they may have to choose between suffering violence and being unable to pay for groceries, electricity, or transportation to work.

Kids

Many parents believe that raising children in a two-parent household is better than raising them alone, regardless of whether the parents have a stable relationship. Some parents do not want their children to lose the love and stability of being raised by two parents. The victim may regard the abuser as a decent parent or fear losing their children's love if the relationship is terminated. Many parents believe that staying in an abusive relationship benefits their children, making it incredibly difficult to leave.

Status of Immigration

Survivors who have moved to western countries confront additional challenges, such as fear of deportation, separation from their children born in the United States, language hurdles, and threats of violence to family members in their home country.

Religion

Many people who are married or in relationships with their abusers believe that leaving the relationship is against their religious beliefs. Even though their religion does not explicitly prohibit divorce, persons of faith may believe that their significant other's behavior is part of a larger plan or a spiritual test. In some cases, exiting the relationship necessitates not just a breakup with the abuser but also a rejection by their religious group.

Fear of Being Found Out

Despite shifting attitudes, many people in many places live in fear of others discovering they are gay, lesbian, bisexual, or transsexual. An abuser in a same-sex or opposite-sex relationship may threaten to reveal the victim's sexuality to family, friends, or coworkers, putting the victim at risk of more violence. If the person fears losing their career, friends or family if they are outed, staying in an abusive relationship may seem like a better alternative.

The Abuser Makes a Promise to Change

While the abuser pledges to change, many victims believe leaving is riskier than staying. Staying in a relationship or marriage when the other person vows to quit being abusive can mean avoiding the breakdown of a marriage or long-term relationship.

Love

It is tempting to believe you can't love an abuser, but abusive relationships are just as complicated as any other. Sometimes the person does not desire to end the relationship; instead, they just want the violence to cease. Even after years of abuse and torment, the victim may still harbor feelings of love for the abuser and a desire to give them "one more chance" to change.

Keep in Mind That Leaving Is a Process

Before permanently divorcing an abusive partner, survivors may leave and return multiple times. According to a study, a victim might take up to seven attempts to permanently leave an abusive partner. Be supportive of someone you suspect is in an abusive relationship. Abusers frequently isolate victims from their friends and family to make them feel they have nowhere to turn to for help. Create a method for safely communicating with the person being mistreated. (If the abuser monitors their cell phone, try e-mail instead.) Locate resources to assist the victim, such as the phone number of a local domestic abuse advocacy program or safety information (Rodgers, 2022).

Remember to be patient with the individual. You may believe the victim should just leave the abuser, but circumstances are rarely that simple. Sometimes leaving is simply not an option, and victims in those situations also require assistance. In many circumstances, leaving the abuser does not cease the violence. People who have left abusive relationships frequently return, and it often takes multiple efforts before a person can successfully and permanently terminate the relationship.

Are There Any Circumstances in Which the Relationship Can Be Saved

What if the abuse isn't that bad? Perhaps you are in a situation where your spouse or loved one is generally good to you, but they can also be manipulative at times. Trying to understand a loved one's struggles with abuse can be very difficult and it isn't something that should be undertaken by any one person alone. Especially if that one person trying to save the relationship is also the actual victim. Sometimes the abuser isn't even aware of the manipulation or hurt that they are imposing and addressing this abuse alone can lead to negative repercussions.

If the abuse is relatively mild, and the victim truly does want to attempt to save the relationship, then the best course of action is to seek professional help from a certified counsellor who specializes in emotional abuse and relationships. A true professional can help diagnose the problems with the abuser and use various methods and recommendations to help improve the situation. They will be able to help assess if the relationship is even savable. Sometimes you may think it can be saved, but the truth is the damage inflicted is just too much to overcome. You must seek a professional's guidance in this situation.

GET READY TO SURMOUNT FLYING MONKEYS

The Flying Monkey Technique is a peculiar exploit in which the narcissist flies out on a self-righteous or cocky tirade against you, leaving the impression that you are the source of his problems. The narcissist may even call your partner or family members (often at great length) to join him in his rant. These "Flying monkeys" are people who actively participate in a narcissist's smear campaign (Warriors, 2021).

Flying monkeys can appear to taunt and mock your efforts when you feel like you are going insane because the world keeps changing around you. They make it clear that despite all your efforts to keep up with everything as it changes, none of it is enough.

Prepare to be chastised by well-meaning individuals. People specializing in narcissistic abuse treatment use the term "flying monkeys" to characterize what is often a dysfunctional web of relationships that emerges when narcissistic victimization is ongoing. Typically, this dysfunctional web includes a larger circle of friends, extended family members, and acquaintances who enable the victim's abuse. The narcissist may use flying monkeys as middlemen, transferring information between parties.

Techniques Used

The flying monkey may use gaslighting techniques, outright aggression, and guilt-tripping to make another person feel miserable and helpless while boosting the narcissist. They are frequently interested in debating the narcissist's point.

Narcissists enjoy having at least one flying monkey because it gives them a sense of significance and helps them appear above the people below them (on both sides) who are embroiled in the drama's negative features (Warriors, 2021).

How Narcissists Work

The narcissist continually recruits their flying monkeys from within the family, including siblings, spouses, and children. Narcissists begin grooming your friends and family the moment they meet you. Initially, the narcissist assesses them and your relationship with them to determine the strength of the bond.

To your friends and family, they may first express their love for you and their belief that you are soul mates. This test will establish whether or not your friends promptly return to you with this information. On the surface, this emerges as kind and loving, but the narcissist is testing your friends' controllability.

Over time, the information they feed your friends and family may have a kernel of truth; nonetheless, the narcissist is now mocking you behind your back. They may emphasize that "Tracy is such a good storyteller that I never know when she is creating something."

This comment builds the framework for later when you begin telling your friends about the narcissist's lies, infidelity, and activities. The seed of mistrust has been planted, and your friends and family will suspect your assertions about narcissists as they progress from good to terrible.

Mission Accomplished

The final level of this flying monkey stage comes after the discard. This is the time when you most need the support of your friends and family, but because of the bond your narcissist has built with them, the narcissist swiftly runs to them and spreads lies about you.

Whatever the narcissist did inaccurately, they will blame you. The narcissist would spread lies about you while emphasizing your great qualities. This cocktail of small cruel lies injures us the most severe since it puts our most protected attributes into question.

Your pals will believe the narcissist's disguise of "playing the victim." The narcissist has chosen the weakest links in your friend network—those who are easiest to influence. These flying monkeys can also spread the smear campaign, further isolating you and preventing you from receiving crucial support. A flying monkey can also convey how much the narcissist adores you and longs for reconciliation (Warriors, 2021). They are simply carrier pigeons carrying out the narcissist's instructions to find you.

This method incorporates your pals in the manipulation to regain you or preserve the impression that they wanted it to work out. You now look to be the villain. Your friends and family members targeted and exploited by narcissists have also been misled.

How To Win Flying Monkey

Flying monkeys are the scapegoats. They are of no value to narcissists and are mere pawns in the game of narcissists, and you are the king or queen. They serve as scapegoats to set up a difficult situation for your friends and family members to defend (Jacobs, 2016). It will automatically put them on the defensive since they have previously defended the narcissist against any allegations made against them. This way, they will think twice before they say anything.

When dealing with flying monkeys, you can do the following to turn them around and transform them into your flying pigs:

- Provide no emotional reaction about the narcissist to them.
- Be your usual sympathetic self around them.
- Give it time.

The narcissist is spouting venom about you to the flying monkeys, and you know this. Well, don't fight back. Don't react at all. Let them hear the lies and let them come to their own conclusions. Don't say a bad word about the narcissist to them. Just withdraw from the narc, focus on other topics with them, and let the flying monkeys study your typical empathic conduct in various contexts.

Recognize and avoid their manipulation and Fear, Obligation, and Guilt (FOG) attempts. Encourage them to clarify their point of view and the reasons behind what they are saying while they're speaking.

Continue to probe them and gather information about what they've been told, what they "know," what they want, and so on, but make no attempt to explain your own actions or explain your side of the story. They have exhibited a lack of interest in what you have to say simply by taking this intervening step, allowing themselves to be entirely misled and controlled by the narc abuser.

You may point out after they've spoken that they've made their own thoughts and conclusions without ever speaking with you alone and hearing your side of the story, which means their thoughts are invalid, and you have no interest in hearing what they have to say.

Time is also your friend since narcissists are con artists, and it's just a matter of time before con artists are exposed. Time always shows who people are at their core. They can't disguise their true selves forever, which is why they go through so many individuals. Narcissists will always expose themselves by their own actions. So, take a step back and let them. You are not required to do anything (Jacobs, 2016).

In conclusion, maintain a level of calm and emotional disengagement throughout the incident. Their goal is to make you feel uncomfortable and disturbed, and if you stay objective, calm, and show little to no emotional engagement, you will have the upper hand, and they will be impotent to influence you. Individuals cannot cause you damage unless you allow them physical or emotional access to you.

GET READY TO DEAL WITH STALKING

Stalking is one of the top reasons people feel unsafe. Stalkers often think they have some relationship with their victims and won't take no for an answer, even if it is communicated. Victims need to talk about and prepare for stalking to know what to do and how to protect themselves when it happens. This section will help you figure out how (Spitzberg and Cupach, 2007).

Stalking is anyone who willfully, maliciously, and repeatedly follows or harasses another person by making a credible threat to place that person in reasonable fear for their safety or the safety of their immediate family.

Unwanted attention is most likely the best way to characterize stalking, and numerous behaviors can be classified as stalking. A counselor may be able to assist you in developing a safety plan. Considerations should be made in the plan for:

- What to do if an assault is currently taking place.
- What to do if you're leaving.
- How to stay safe after you've left.

Talk to an Advocate

It is crucial to pursue the help of a confidential victim advocate who can help you understand your rights and options and create a safety plan for yourself. You do not have to give your name or any information that would make you vulnerable to being identified as the victim of a crime or wrongful act. If you are in immediate danger and are feeling unsafe and want to prevent yourself from being stalked, consider getting a restraining order.

Twenty-four hours of emergency response is available seven days a week in case of urgent matters, such as a sexual assault that occurred in the last five days or help with emergency shelter in case of domestic violence. By appointment, a victim advocate can meet with you during business hours. If you have a serious problem, you may schedule an appointment for the same day.

Forms of Stalking

An abuser can continue to pressurize and influence over a survivor even after the survivor has left a relationship that was pegged to domestic violence. The act of stalking can take many different forms. Some instances of stalking take the form of threatening phone calls and emails, while other instances take the form of leaving flowers and chocolates on a car window (Spitzberg and Cupach, 2007).

Stalking can also take the form of leaving flowers and chocolates in a car window. A person can file a report and seek additional assistance to obtain protection if they believe they are the target of stalking. Two options are available: one is to seek a restraining order, and the other is to look for alternative housing, such as a shelter for victims of domestic violence.

What To Do in Case of Stalking

After leaving an abusive relationship, a person who has been a domestic violence victim should heed experts' advice and take additional safety precautions, as there is a greater risk of physical harm (Rodgers, 2022). If a survivor has a restraining order, it is absolutely necessary for copies of the order to be made and kept at their place of employment, their residence, their educational institution, and/or on their person.

The victim needs to report the crime to the appropriate authorities if the perpetrator of the abuse continues to harass or stalk the victim. Criminal prosecution is possible for the offense known as stalking (Spitzberg and Cupach, 2007). The actions of the stalker can have a significant impact on the victim, who may experience heightened anxiety, increased vigilance, anger, and other negative emotions as a result.

The person who stalks them is frequently someone the victim knows, and the two of them may have even had a romantic relationship in the past. Victims of stalking may try to handle the situation on their own before reporting the unwanted behavior, which may cause them to delay reporting it for weeks, months, or even years.

If you are experiencing undesired behaviors from a known or unknown someone that are causing you to feel afraid or nervous, there are some things you can do:

- Call 911 if you are in urgent danger.
- Believe in your intuition. Don't underestimate the threat. If you feel unsafe, you most likely are.
- You should take threats seriously. The danger increases when the stalker discusses suicide or murder or when the victim attempts to leave or end the contact.
- Contact an advocate who can help you understand your rights and alternatives and assist you in developing a safety plan. To discover more about how to contact a confidential advocate at CARE, see the "Talk to an Advocate" section.
- Do not connect with the stalker or reply to contact attempts.
- Keep documentation of the stalking. Note the duration, date, time, and location when the stalker follows you or contacts you. Keep all emails, texts, phone calls, letters, and notes. Photograph anything the stalker damages, as well as any injuries the stalker causes. Request that witnesses write down what they witnessed.
- Create a police report. The stalker may have violated other crimes by attacking you or stealing or destroying your belongings.
- Consider obtaining a court order directing the stalker to stay away from you.

- Inform your family, friends, housemates, and coworkers about the stalking and request their assistance.

Physical Violence

If your spouse was physically violent during the relationship, they might continue to be so once the relationship is over. And if physical violence escalates during a relationship, it is best to presume it will continue to escalate once the relationship ends. There are other red flags to be aware of.

"Use extra caution when leaving if there was physical violence while pregnant or in public, strangling, threats with a weapon, or words like, 'If you go, I'll kill myself,'" they warn. "Those kinds of behaviors demonstrate that they are unconcerned about the repercussions." Abusive partners with military or police training make the situation more dangerous due to their access to weapons and ability to cause maximum physical harm.

Pay attention to non-physical signals, too.

Of course, even if they were not physically violent, abusers may resort to violence once the relationship ends. When leaving a relationship, use caution if your partner exhibits any indicators of controlling conduct, such as financial abuse, sexual coercion, isolating you from loved ones, verbal abuse, and gaslighting.

If you are undergoing any of these issues, it is essential to speak with someone knowledgeable about safety planning and with the resources to offer you the assistance you require. Call a hotline or go to a shelter to speak with someone who can walk you through all of the options for safely leaving.

GET READY TO DEAL WITH BEGGING, GUILT TRIPPING, AND PLAYING THE VICTIM

If toxic individuals were ingestible, they would be accompanied by a strong warning and secure packaging to prevent accidental contact.

Unfortunately, families are not immune to the corrosive effects of a toxic relationship.

Though family and relationships can be difficult at times, they were never meant to be destroyed. Every relationship has flaws, and none of them come with a constant glow of sunshine, goodness, and beautiful things. Fights will occur from time to time in any normal relationship, and things will be said, done, forgiven, and then rehashed at strategic times. They will, however, feel nurturing and life-giving for the most part. They won't hurt, at the very least.

Why Do Toxic People Do Toxic Things?

Control is what toxic people crave. Not the kind of caring, healthy control that wants to make everyone secure and happy but the kind that shrinks and diminishes people.

They do everything they can to maintain people small and manageable, which will manifest in criticism, judgment, and tyranny—whatever it takes to keep someone in their place. The more you try to leave "your position," the more a toxic person will use poisonous behavior to drag you back into the narrow box they believe you belong in.

Poisonous people likely develop their behavior in childhood by witnessing others' toxic behavior or being overpraised without being taught empathy. In a toxic relationship, respect, kindness, and compassion are also lacking, but a toxic person lacks concern for others and can't see beyond their own desires.

Toxic individuals choose open, nice people with lovely, lavish hearts because they are less likely to abandon. Even the strongest people can end up in a poisonous relationship, and the longer they stay, the smaller, less confident, and more wounded they become.

Toxic people know that non-toxic people in toxic relationships will never stop attempting to improve it. It is expected and non-toxic people will work to make the relationship work, giving the toxic person control.

Why Are Toxic Relationships So Destructive?

Love is circular in any good relationship; when you offer love, it returns. When what returns is scrappy, stingy intent disguised as love, it will eventually leave you little and depleted, falling wildly, terrifyingly short of where anyone is supposed to be.

Healthy people appreciate the support and progress of others they care about, even if it means adapting slightly. It can be difficult when an individual in a system changes, whether it's a two-person relationship or a large family. Even the most loving and healthy relationships can be impacted by feelings of jealousy, inadequacy, and insecurity in response to someone's growth or satisfaction (Logue, 2019). We are all susceptible to experiencing the typical, tumultuous emotions that come with being human.

The distinction is that healthy families and relationships will work through difficult times. Unhealthy people will blame, manipulate, and lie—whatever it takes to get things back to how they've always been with the toxic person in charge.

Why Toxic Relationships Will Never Change

No matter how strong and self-reliant they are, you can easily lead reasonable people to believe that if they could only locate the switch, do less, do more, control it, adjust it, the relationship would be fine. The harsh reality is that it would have happened by now if anything were to change.

Toxic people can and will change, but it is extremely improbable. Nothing anyone else can do will change their minds. There will almost certainly be shattered people, broken hearts, and destroyed relationships around them, but the devastation will always be blamed on someone else. There will be no remorse, regret, or understanding, and any broken relationship is more likely to intensify their harmful behavior.

Why Are Toxic Relationships So Hard to Leave

If you try to leave a toxic individual, things may worsen before they get better, but they will always get better. Always. Few things in a relationship increase feelings of insecurity or a need for control more than when someone challenges familiar, old behavior or attempts to break away from old, established routines. When a person's characteristic moves entail manipulation, deception, criticism, or any other toxic behavior, they will use even more of their regular harmful behavior to get the relationship (or the person) back to an acceptable level.

When something doesn't appear to be working, individuals will always do more of what used to work, even if that behavior is the source of the problem. It's something we all do. If you are naturally open and generous, you will likely give more of yourself, offer more support, and be more loving to get things back on track in a relationship when things don't feel right.

Leaving a toxic relationship can feel like ripping barbed wire with your bare unprotected hands. The more you continue doing it, the more it hurts, so you stop tearing for a while until you realize it is the barbed wire—the relationship—that hurts, and whether you tear at it or not do it, it won't stop cutting into you.

Consider it this way: assume that all relationships and families share a space. The shape of that space in a healthy one will be fluid and open to change, with plenty of room for individuals to grow and move to accommodate each other's growth and flight.

That shape is tight and unyielding for a bad family or poisonous relationship. There is no room for suppleness, bending, or expansion. Everyone has a clearly defined space, which may be small and severely boxed for some. When one family member begins to break free from the shape, the entire family feels their particular parts change.

The shape may fluctuate, and items may feel vulnerable, weakened, or frightening. This is normal, but toxic people will go to any length to return the area to its original state. Frequently, this will include crumpling the ones who are shifting to fit their area again.

People trapped in a toxic relationship may sometimes forego growth and change to return to the inflexible, tiny space that a toxic person manipulates them into out of a sense of love and tragically mistaken loyalty. It will be obvious when this has occurred due to the soul-sucking sadness of being back there in the muck with people (or individuals) who make you feel so horrible to be with.

The One Truth That Matters

Follow growth or nourishment. It may mean walking away from parents, siblings, brothers, and friends, but you may do it with love and leave the door open for when they can meet you on your terms. Set limitations with grace and kindness, then let the toxic person choose. Boundaries shouldn't be used for spite or manipulation or to end a relationship. They show people your entrance with power and confidence. If the relationship ends, it is not because you lack love or loyalty, but because the toxic person doesn't treat you well. They choose to do so.

You can define the terms under which someone can be close to you, but it is up to them to respect those restrictions. If they ignore your requests, they won't be with you, which doesn't mean you'll ignore them. Toxic people have relationship standards, which they may not mention but include tolerating ridicule, judgement, criticism, oppression, lying, and manipulation. No relationship is worth that, and declining anything weakening is okay.

True friends and family want you to be entire. Sometimes choosing health and wholeness means avoiding what would break and malnourish your spirit. Young, defenseless, and dependent on grownups, you had little control over who you let close. But that's not how your life is right now. You have the last say and control over the terms of your relationships and the individuals you associate with.

There is no need to choose poisonous people simply because they are relatives. If they are poisonous, the plain truth is that they didn't pick you and have selected a version of you that is inferior to the person you would be without them.

How To Behave When Someone Tries to Guilt You

When someone tries to guilt you, you may feel stuck. Some situations are harder to get out of than others. Such as, if someone has authority over you or is playing your heartstrings, you always have a voice. Going against our culture's teaching that it's disrespectful to say "no" might be uncomfortable. It is not always disrespectful to say "no," and the person trying to guilt trip is rude.

Tools can help you say "no" effectively. Putting any of the following methods into action may help you face down a guilt trip:

Don't take it personally

Someone trying to guilt you may say you are the only one who can help them. Maybe your work skills or attitude make you the "ideal person" to help them. Whatever it is, it is helpful to remember that you're not the only one who can help them.

Jen Smith of *HuffPost* adds, "The goal of a guilt trip is to make it personal, so you submit." Even if you could help someone, you don't have to; you are not the only one they'll ask. You are not the only one they can ask for aid, especially if they use guilt instead of a clear request.

Express how their behavior makes you feel

Your feelings and voice count, especially when someone tries to make you feel bad about something you shouldn't. You may tell someone their request makes you uncomfortable, says Guy Winch, Ph.D., of Psychology Today. A true friend will apologize, and someone who is guilt-tripping you is unlikely to change their behavior.

Put the ball back in their court.

Winch suggests reminding the guilter that their needs are essential and that they must take responsibility. You can acknowledge some-one's needs without handling them yourself. Support your co-worker's concerns, but place the onus on them to pull it all together rather than volunteering you for the job.

Practice standing up for yourself

We try to prevent bad emotions. When we feel guilty, we may feel uncomfortable and wish to change our emotions immediately. Guilt is a natural emotion you should embrace. Saying "no" and feeling guilty is normal; it doesn't make you a bad person.

GET READY TO DEAL WITH YOUR OWN FEAR OF BEING ALONE

It is a sad truth that many refuse to face: we all dread being alone. Whether you call it loneliness or solitude, most of us would rather avoid it at any cost—and that means sticking with a relationship, even when it would be better to break up.

Finding genuine connections with others is the only way to stop feeling this way; if your current relationship precludes this, then you need to make a change. Oftentimes the benefits of being alone will outweigh the risks and abuse one may suffer from while styling in a rotten relationship.

How does it affect relationships?

A partnership where one person isn't there isn't likely to bring joy or fulfilment. It's possible to prolong a relationship like this for years, where neither party is likely to be satisfied. One of the major problems with this kind of thinking is that the relationship limps on with no end in sight.

Eventually, it will become obvious that one individual no longer loves the other or never has. This may manifest as a lack of affection or eye contact, and it may also manifest in larger ways, such as conflicts or excessive time away from home. It is feasible to fake it, but it won't go well. In such cases, the space between the two persons widens until they inevitably break apart.

Making Changes

Breakups hurt. Breaking up with someone is a loss, even if you know the relationship has no future. Even if the change is painful, we can find more enjoyment by weathering it.

Putting some distance between relationships can help us find out what we desire. If you've been in a relationship, it might be helpful to focus on what you like, what makes you happy, your values, and the direction you want your life to follow. Knowing these causes can help you choose the appropriate person for your future relationship, as you'll be able to locate someone who shares your values and is compatible in other ways.

Take time to build non-romantic relationships. Having a support network is important for self-esteem. Visiting friends and family will remind you that you're not alone. Creating new relationships—by joining social clubs or contacting old friends—will help you establish independence, a vital aspect of any healthy love relationship.

Now, about loneliness. Although the aforementioned is crucial for a healthy mental attitude and self-esteem, being single can still seem lonely. Even when doing everything perfectly, you'll miss the romantic relationship. Accepting this as part of life is sometimes the best option. We all must endure some sadness to achieve our goals.

Ending a Toxic Relationship

What types of toxic relationships should you end? Toxicity isn't restricted to romantic interactions. Toxic people include:

- Family members
- Co-workers
- Friends
- Neighbors
- Business partners
- Schoolmates

Step carefully. It's valuable. You are valuable. Don't rush.

Step Out of Denial

The first cause of action in resolving any problem or conflict is confronting it squarely. This is especially true when it comes to exiting harmful relationships. Admitting you are in a toxic relationship may appear to be a tiny step. But it is quite large. You are crossing a chasm from denial to acceptance.

You've got this!

Science is on your side. Many studies have shown that sustaining a toxic relationship has negative health consequences. A 2021 study, for example, discovered that experiences of being harassed, bullied, or ostracized in a hazardous workplace might lead to (van Heugten, 2021):

- Stress
- Burnout
- Depression
- Anxiety

Keep a Log of Emotions

Writing about your feelings may be the last thing on your mind. You might be too tense to concentrate. Furthermore, you may be concerned that putting it down will make you feel worse.

Expressive writing is a term used by psychologists to describe writing down your feelings. They also agree that you may feel more worried, scared, or upset shortly after writing.

However, you will likely realize both mental and physical benefits within a few weeks. Expressive writing has many health benefits, including fewer healthcare visits for the stress-enhanced immune system, lower blood pressure, enhanced lung function, fewer hospital days, and a greater sense of well-being.

Identify the perks

Your unhealthy relationship might possibly have advantages. So, grab your journal and jot them down. Do you recognize any of these?

- We split the bills. I wouldn't have had the money to live alone.
- She's like family. At the very least, she babysits on occasion.
- Sure, my boss is poisonous. At the very least, I know what to expect.
- I'm in my sixties, and everything is familiar to me. How might I restart my life?
- Make a list of your motivations and benefits. Check to see if the benefits are truly worth the cost.

Hint: They most likely aren't. Seeing things in black and white on paper can help.

Fill the Holes

Voids will pop up in your life after the rewards are gone; now is the time to plan how to fill them up. Say one of the positives of your terrible relationship is possessing a home. You might start looking for alternative housing arrangements, even if it involves bunking up with a friend or family member for a short while.

If shared funds are the perk, now could be the moment to become open to a second career or short-term gig. If companionship, or even love, is a reward, remember that there are other fish in the sea. Most importantly, start doing the things you enjoy that your relationship hindered you from doing.

Surround Yourself with Positive Friends

Refresh your cache by considering which friends or family members can help you (and you, them!). Even one person is sufficient; they will inspire you and show you what life may be like outside of a poisonous relationship. You may also consider visiting a therapist or signing up for a support group.

These folks will stick by you even if the relationship ends. You'll need them for emotional support, job placement assistance, and suggestions for a new place to live. According to research, the quality of your relationships can impact your immune system and your motivation, mood, and coping skills (Kemeny, 2003). Social support can even reduce your chances of acquiring health problems such as heart disease, cancer, depression, addiction, and more.

Drop a Note to Yourself

Among everyone in your support network, there is one person you absolutely must have on your side: you!

You are the one who is the most familiar with you and has been with you the longest. Try writing down all of your wisdom, love, and compassion, sealing it in an envelope, and mailing it to yourself. If you can't find enough self-love to do so right now, that's fine. Try composing the letter under the guise of a buddy who is the most sympathetic person you can imagine.

Treat Yourself

Rewarding yourself for making a change for the better is acceptable. Reward yourself with something you genuinely enjoy. Maybe it is reading a book alone or obtaining your favorite drink. Of course, this strategy might be abused and turn into distraction or escapism, which is not something you want to do. Escapism often plays a role in relationships after people rebound from painful breakups. It is easier to seek solace in someone else than to deal with the situation on their own. Being wanted and desired by someone helps mask the pain of a breakup. The individual may appear to have escaped dealing with the pain head-on, but in reality, the wound has not been properly addressed or healed. It just lays dormant, throbbing silently until one day, it resurfaces in a new way.

People escape from other things in their lives, as well. For example, socially, people tend to avoid public places. Many people remain in passionless jobs because they are afraid of failure or because they are afraid they will not find something better elsewhere. Some people avoid challenges because they fear perceived "pain" and "suffering." Others avoid their pasts in order to avoid remembering their deepest sorrows. People who avoid their issues because they think they have no strength to face them. There are even some who spend their whole lives trying to escape from their issues.

However, accomplishing something difficult and then rewarding yourself might boost your motivation. A research review from 2011 says rewards can boost motivation and help you achieve your goals. According to the study, neuronal connections between reinforcement and learning are among the oldest in the human brain (Remschmidt, 2011). If rewards have worked throughout history, they can undoubtedly work for you!

Heal the Guilt

You may feel guilty for various reasons when you quit a toxic relationship. Perhaps you are feeling guilty because you:

- Stayed in the relationship for too long
- Hurt the other person
- Believe the relationship may have impacted your children

Whatever the cause of your guilt, the first step toward healing is self-forgiveness. Forgiveness can benefit you both emotionally and physically. According to Johns Hopkins Medicine, forgiveness can (Forgiveness: Your Health Depends on It, 2021):

- Decrease heart attack chances
- Reduce blood pressure
- Improve cholesterol levels
- Reduce levels of anxiety, depression, and stress

Repeat Affirmations

Affirmations can be extremely effective transformation agents. For example, if you want to feel strong, tell yourself, "I am strong." Of course, you'll need to take action as well! Regular self-affirmation practice truly affects the brain. MRI pictures from a 2016 study show that those who practice self-affirmation have more active brain networks.

Allow for Some Rest

Most relationship experts agree that one of the most important things you can do after any breakup is to give yourself time to heal. This is particularly true following a terrible relationship. After closing that chapter, take as much time as you need to breathe and enjoy life again.

Are You Afraid to Leave a Relationship?

You're more alone than you realize. Your concern has come true. Formally being alone would only cement something that has been your reality for a long time and, paradoxically, would help you end your loneliness and unbearable anguish.

You can't eliminate your emotional loneliness unless you experience a period of practical loneliness, which you know (but are scared of). Dinner alone is nothing compared to feeling existentially misunderstood by your partner. Someone who won't understand is worse than an empty chair.

You spend a lot of energy defending yourself from legitimate hope by relying on general truths: All love is flawed, and honeymoons end. Change "lovers" to "movies" or "vacation locations" to see this self-serving hyperbole. As with films and resorts, there are no perfect lovers. This isn't an excuse to never change the channel or deny that Birmingham and Lake Como are different. There is a "better" and a "worse," a truth that is no less true for being difficult to comprehend.

It is worse to be publicly together but personally alone, just as it is better to be permitted to grieve than forced to grin while burning inside.

What's holding us back is something unexpected in the background: We don't trust or like ourselves, and we feel unworthy and humiliated (it is from infancy). Self-hatred causes our inability to escape. If we were on our own side, we'd deserve and be able to claim much more.

SURMOUNT THE CHALLENGES WORKSHEET

Because attempting to leave an abusive relationship means having to scale several challenges and opposition, it's only wise to be prepared.

Have you tried to leave this abusive relationship before?

....

....

....

Why have you not been able to leave?

....

....

....

Do you feel like you'll be able to move on with your life if you go no contact and completely break off ties with this person?

....

....

....

What is your biggest fear about completely cutting off ties with this person?

....

....

....

What's the biggest thing that scares you about going no-contact with this person?

....

....

....

If you had the opportunity to take all of these fears back, would you still take them back and pursue?

....

....

....

Are there any unresolved issues between yourself and the other party(s) involved in the situation they need to deal with during your recovery process and beyond?

....

....

....

4

BREAKING FREE FROM NARCISSISM

Narcissism is a prominent disorder with an insidious presence, often taking the form of extreme self-absorption and a lack of concern for others. Despite this, it can be difficult for people struggling with narcissism to see themselves as having a problem or even realize that they have narcissistic tendencies. The difficulty in pinpointing narcissistic tendencies can result in feelings of frustration and helplessness on the part of those trying to break free from the disorder.

Emotional abuse comes in different shades, but narcissism is perhaps one of the darkest and most difficult to get through. This chapter thoroughly gives insight into surviving narcissistic abuse, breaking free, and letting go for good.

WHAT IS NARCISSISM?

When we talk about narcissism, many attribute it to people being full of themselves. While this is true in some ways, narcissism is a personality disorder. It is a severe psychological disorder that involves attaching excessive importance to oneself. Narcissism doesn't even have to do with genuine self-love. More appropriately, narcissists are in love with a non-existent image of themselves that exists in their heads. They resort to falling in love with this image since it allows them to escape the feeling of insecurity that plagues them deep down. However, it takes more effort to keep up with this false sense of majesty. This is why a narcissistic personality involves a dysfunctional attitude and behavior.

This sense of importance is so excessive and in no way the same as ordinary people. Those with this disorder are characterized by an inability to think of others, let alone put themselves in other people's shoes. This is coupled with an abnormal need for admiration or acknowledgment.

As a result of their excessive need for admiration, they are usually selfish, manipulative, cocky, arrogant, and demanding. This individual exists in almost all social circles you encounter in life. Parents, children, romantic partners, colleagues, and other people can all manifest this trait. This leads to serious issues, more severe than someone who attaches a little more importance to themselves.

People with this disorder have this false belief that they are better and superior to all others. This belief, however, has no factual basis. It manifests in the way they interact and relate to others. They are drawn to gifted people or those that can act as a source of fuel for them. People with NPD need this association to supply their damaged or fragile self-esteem. This is why they are always on a quest for attention as proof their peers hold them in high esteem.

People with NPD also do not take criticism lightly. Even constructive criticism does not go down well with them, and they cannot accept the fact that they are wrong or faulty. As a result, they feel humiliated, injured, or attacked when criticized.

In understanding narcissistic personality disorder, it is vital to know the tenets that define the disorder. A few of these are:

- Authority
- Self-sufficiency (believing your strength and wisdom got you here)
- Exhibitionism
- Superiority
- Vanity
- Entitlement
- Exploitation

These characteristics form the foundation of the disturbing personality found in a narcissist. They have a high affinity for accolades while promoting themselves, which only isolates them more, even though they long for approval and inclusion deep down.

TYPES OF NARCISSISTS

More often than not, the word narcissist is commonly used these days. You hear it in the news headlines, in day-to-day conversation, etc. Besides, many people believe that a narcissist is someone who thinks so excessively of themselves, that others matter a little to them.

When you consider how narcissism is used, you will think there is a specific pattern to which all narcissism conforms. In reality, narcissism occurs on a spectrum with healthy self-esteem on one end and NPD on the other. As a result, no two narcissists are rarely alike, and they come in diverse personalities with various modes of revealing their majesty. Besides, the way they affect self-esteem also differs.

Here are the most extreme types of narcissists you might encounter. They could be of any gender (even though it is common to the male gender):

Overt Narcissism

They are loud, always want to be heard, are in control, and are never wrong. They are the most common. They have this feeling of knowing more and better than others. As a result, whether welcomed or not, they will voice their opinion and expect people to agree and go along with them. Things must always go their way, and they are not ashamed to say it.

They are bullies that believe in painting others badly to make themselves look like the good guy. They lash out at others and humiliate them without guilt. They are known to attack people by mocking and belittling them. They are gifted at coining words to downgrade their victims, so they feel useless and worthless as humans.

The Covert Narcissist

On the other hand, the covert narcissist puts up a false image in a bid to deceive people. In other words, they will present themselves as kind, loving, and liberal, but don't be fooled. They have grasped the art of manipulation to get what they want.

They are usually found in positions of authority, such as politicians, teachers, leaders, and so on. Since they are masters at deceiving people, they can pretend and put up any front to get what they want.

The Grandiose Narcissist

This is a type we are more familiar with. The grandiose narcissist considers themselves the most successful, more important than anyone else. He derives pleasure in blowing his trumpet and makes himself feel more relevant than necessary. They do this to make you jealous.

The grandiose narcissist feels his duty in the world is to accomplish great things. Truly, if you meet a serious and hardworking type, the achievement could be in sync with their ambitions. As a result, you have zero choice but to admire them.

They love having the spotlight on them, so you will encounter any challenge to outshine them with stern disapproval. They will increase their efforts to ensure you don't surpass them.

The Status Antagonist

These types of narcissists believe they are not worthy unless they receive the validation of others. They strive intensely for power, money, and social status with little or no sense of self. This social status helps keep their self-confidence intact. They use their achievement as a measuring stick to judge other people.

They are pretty smart in pursuing their goals and passions. As a result, they strive for headship positions like a chairman or president, and they only settle for second in command as a last resort.

The Narcissistic Winner

For the narcissistic winner, everything is competition, and they have an extreme desire to compete in everything. This is not about competition in sports, academics, and careers; it also involves day-to-day activities like friendship, spirituality, parenting, and more.

These are the kind of people that get jealous when good things happen to their friends. Since life, in general, is a competition to them, they believe they are more qualified for the good things. They resort to belittling others' achievements to make themselves feel better.

UNDERSTANDING THE NARCISSIST'S TACTICS

An understanding of the mind of a narcissist helps one interpret their actions. Even though they appear strong and confident, they are weak and predictable. This is why a careful examination of narcissists' behavior shows that their life follows a pattern, making them less enticing.

Watch out for the following patterns.

Narcissists are Cunning and Masters at Earning Peoples'

Narcissists always know just the right words to say, how to captivate people and therefore, you need to know this as you deal with them. Remember, these people are masters of deception and know how to seem caring and make you feel important, all in a bid to get close to you.

From a distance, a narcissist is playful, exciting, and lively. It is easy to fall in love with them as they are master seducers with a slew of romantic gestures to shower unsuspecting victims.

Once they have you, it is hard to back out. Your life and relationship will likely be subjected to abuse, trauma, and objectification until it ends. They won't show you their true colors until it's time because they know it will just turn you off. Because of this, they put so much effort into hiding their true selves.

As you proceed in the relationship, you find yourself reluctant to leave and have difficulty believing your partner is the problem (Thompson, Bonomi, Anderson, Reid, Dimer, Carrell, and Rivara, 2006). This makes you always second guess the things you say or do, which would make anyone go crazy.

They Deceive Without Remorse

Honesty is not in the DNA of a narcissist. They can twist any event to the degree that better suits their selfish needs. Bear in mind that they do not think of their lies as lies. For example, if they claim you are suffocating them in the relationship, they do not mind telling everyone you know that you are too clingy.

Putting others down means nothing to a narcissist. They target your self-esteem with their insults and abusive words so that your subconscious starts accepting them. With time, you start to look up to them for approval. People outside won't see it or them for who they are.

They Have a Deep Sense of Insecurity

Even though narcissists love manipulating and putting others down, true happiness is always far from their grasp. This is because anyone truly happy does not need to bring others down, and they are a weak, helpless individual with the consciousness that they lack healthy human interaction.

They may not say it, but they are aware of their brokenness. Deep down, this person sees the joy and satisfaction from everyday interactions and relationships that elude them. Oh, what a lonely place to be.

Rather than looking inward for growth and self-development, they prefer to depend on others for their source of strength. This ultimately forms a pattern of terrible habits.

HOW TO RECOGNIZE A NARCISSIST

Demands Constant Admiration

In the same way, a motor vehicle engine needs constant fuel to keep running, a narcissist's sense of superiority needs a steady supply of recognition. This is different from the occasional compliment that is enough for normal people. You must constantly feed their ego, so they like to be around people they can feed off.

They are fond of having only one-sided relationships in which all that matters is what they can get from it. To make matters worse, they see this attention as a right and react vehemently should the focus diminish.

Lack of Empathy

You do not have to lack empathy to be a narcissist. However, when someone lacks empathy, alongside a sense of exploitation and entitlement, they could be a narcissist. Take note of how they react during the hardship of others. Do they appear insensitive to that person's plight?

Some things that demonstrate a lack of empathy are rudeness, violating your boundaries, taking calls during a conversation, etc. These examples alone do not mean someone is a narcissist.

A Sense of Entitlement

In other words, they act like the universe revolves around them. Not only are they special, but they deserve to be treated better than everyone else. They do not count themselves as subject to rules or boundaries, which is why they feel they can push boundaries without thinking of the consequences.

When people with NPD are wrong, every other person causes it, and the law isn't right. You are supposed to put their needs above yours; for instance, only cook their favorite meal or go out for dinner when they feel like it. Since all they care about is getting what they want, such a relationship will be one-sided. And to them, you are merely a pawn they can use to boost their self-esteem.

Exploiting Others

To a narcissist, people in their life are objects or tools to meet their selfish needs. They are not evolved to the point of identifying with the feelings of others, and this makes it easy for them to take advantage of others without remorse. They do not care about the effect their behavior has on others. And if you are bold enough to point it out, expect them to lash out in a very negative way.

If you are unlucky to be in a relationship with one, they will always place their needs, feelings, and wants before yours.

Forms a Pattern of Intimidation, Bully, and Belittling Others

You are a threat to the narcissist if you are better than them. People who stand up to them and confront them are a threat. As a means to defend themselves, they resort to ridicule and scorn. They have to put others down in a bid to soothe their ego.

This might be insults, bullying, or threatening to force a person to back down. It can also be a dismissive way to show that the person means nothing to them.

Excessive Feelings of Superiority

Narcissists are fond of putting others down, talking badly about people in charge, because deep inside, they know they are inferior. To determine if someone is a narcissist, watch how they treat others, such as gatemen, waiters, and bartenders. They hold people of honor in high esteem to get on their good side while they are critical to the people that serve them.

A narcissist never believes they are wrong and must be right in all circumstances. Even if you argue, they will twist and confuse your brain until you succumb.

Watch out for more than three traits described above before passing someone off as a narcissist. An individual could manifest any of the signs above and not be narcissistic.

WHY IT IS DIFFICULT TO BREAK FREE FROM A NARCISSIST

If you have experienced narcissistic abuse, you know how traumatic and upsetting it can be. Narcissists are masters of manipulation who will do their best to retain control over you, even after the relationship has ended. The reason it is hard to break free from a narcissist is because they want you to feel worthless and without options, which ensures that they will always be your only choice. They will make every effort to maintain your sense of dependence on them and prevent you from moving on.

When attempting to end a relationship with a narcissist, you are confronted with several harsh realities. The narcissist is analogous to the narcotic, and our commitment to the narc is analogous to drug addiction. I heard somewhere that narcissists are addicting. Why is this the case? There are numerous reasons for this. One of them is that they are larger than life. Narcissists are not regular people, and their relationships are anything but typical.

It is quite tough to break off from a narcissistic relationship. To do so, you must first recognize basic truths about the reality of your situation. You aren't interacting with an average person here, and you are not breaking out from a harmless union. You must recognize that the narc is what you require on a fundamental, unconscious, visceral level.

Do not underestimate the strength of your feelings for the narcissist. Every human being wishes to feel significant, cherished, and secure. The narcissistic relationship responds to these fundamental demands. There is no stronger desire than that which a narcissist can convey. Once we become entangled in their web, escaping is extremely difficult due to the narcissist's ability to tap into and appeal to our intrinsic, felt needs.

Unfortunately, those of us trapped in their web learn to realize that the gift of narcissistic love is a gift that never ends. We scarcely recognize ourselves after being in a relationship with a narcissist for an extended period, and we devolve into a hollowed-out shell of who we once were.

1. A narcissist can make us feel important.

It's no surprise that narcissistic people expect a lot from their friends. According to one recent study, narcissism is "motivated by insecurity, not an exaggerated sense of self." As a result, while they may project confidence in the public, much of their identity is frail in private. While we are near a narcissist, we might be a tool they use to elevate or improve their self-worth. They may believe that if their self-image cracks, everything will crumble. Consequently, we may feel very bad about leaving a narcissist.

2. Narcissists can make us feel unique.

Even though a narcissist might take up a lot of space in our lives and keep us in their shadow, staying close to them can make us feel like we're basking in their warmth. We would lose the spotlight that shines on them if we lost them. We may be hesitant to leave because we fear losing the sense of uniqueness we have obtained by being related to them.

3. We may feel as if we are losing our identity.

Because we have taken on so many of the other person's issues and so much of their identity in a narcissistic relationship, leaving them may feel like giving up a part of ourselves. We can feel lost without them if they have come to represent the center of our universe. As a result, even when the relationship has dark features, we believe that we will be fully in the dark if we leave (Staff, 2022).

4. Narcissists can wreak havoc on our self-esteem.

Unfortunately, we all have a part of ourselves that questions and reduces who we are. Every one of us has a "critical inner voice" that tells us we are unworthy or unpleasant in various ways. Being with narcissists might sometimes make us feel better about ourselves because we enjoy being chosen by someone with such inflated self-esteem. Our significant other may also build us up, making us feel special because they would only be with someone exceptional.

5. We've become addicted to push and pull.

Relationships with narcissists are fraught with highs and lows. Mania is a common element of every kind of narcissistic love. Narcissism is frequently coupled with a "gaming love style." Our companion may make us feel like we are the center of their universe for one minute. That said, we may appear to be their last priority. When we are present for them, a narcissist may pay us little attention, but when we are absent, they will face us with strong emotions.

This dynamic can make us feel overwhelmed, confused, or upset, but it can also get us addicted to it. The other person's push and pull can make them more appealing. We may believe we require that passionate, exhilarating love to feel worthy of ourselves. As one narcissist's girlfriend said, "If I can get him to adore me, then I am genuinely special."

Because we feel lost and as if we have nothing without the other person, we may stay with them and try to reclaim their attention. This dynamic can be especially appealing to people who grew up with an insecure attachment pattern in which they believed they couldn't have their needs satisfied or didn't feel regularly nourished or loved. In all its sparkling abundance, the occasional reinforcement they receive from a narcissist can appear to be something they must do to feel okay about themselves.

6. Narcissists can reinvent our past.

We are drawn to narcissists often for historical reasons, and these explanations are frequently shaped by our early interaction and attachment tendencies. Committing to someone with comparable self-centered traits would feel familiar if we had parents who required our assurance or had us take care of them.

If we grew up feeling frightened that we couldn't obtain the love or attention we required from our primary caregiver, staying in a relationship where we feel this same sense of desperation can be something we are instinctively driven to. These dynamics may be unpleasant, but they are well-known, and we are compelled to imitate them because they are the models we are taught about how relationships should function.

Because the dynamics that drive us to narcissistic relationships are often rooted in our internal habits and personal histories, breaking free from a narcissist may necessitate some self-reflection. We may be suffering from our sense of self or have been hurt in previous relationships, which causes us to get locked in unpleasant patterns with our current partner.

We can learn a lot about ourselves by examining what attracts us to narcissistic people, what dynamics they repeat, and what negative self-concepts they reinforce. We might then begin to question such patterns and beliefs. We can break out from relationships that limit and harm us. Finally, we may position ourselves in the future to choose better, more meaningful, and equal partnerships.

BREAKING FREE FROM NARCISSISM WORKSHEET

Emotional abuse comes in different shades, but narcissism is perhaps one of the darkest and most difficult to get through.

Who is the narcissist in your life?

....

....

....

Describe their major tactics that you've recognized.

....

....

....

Do they do anything that you can't understand?

....

....

....

Do they have any needs or wants in their life that seem unreasonable to you?

....

....

....

Have they ever done or said things which were unreasonable to you? Were there any other people involved in the situation who thought so too?

....

....

....

Have you been involved with someone who has a sense of entitlement better than most other people?

....

....

....

How do you feel about cutting yourself off from the narcissist, and why don't you feel ready to go no contact yet?

....

....

....

What will my life look like if I continue to stay in this abusive relationship? What will it look like 1 year from now? What about 5 years from now? And 10 years from now?

....

....

....

What would my life look like, if I decided to leave this abusive relationship and take the steps necessary to recover? What will it look like 1 year from now? What about 5 years from now? And 10 years from now?

....

....

....

5

HOW TO BREAK FREE FROM TOXIC FAMILY RELATIONSHIPS

Family is a complicated thing. Friendships can be difficult to maintain, but family relationships are in an entire category. The family will always be there, and you can't get rid of them as easily as you could pack up your belongings and leave town.

But some families also have toxic relationships that can ruin your life, even if they are not directly hurting you.

THE RIGORS OF A DYSFUNCTIONAL FAMILY

When you have an abusive family, it is hard to tell what part of your issues are related to the relationship and what would still be there without them. Even in the more subtle cases, having a toxic relationship with a parent or sibling can ruin your self-esteem, make you feel guilty all the time, and bring up feelings of inadequacy.

Additionally, being around somebody who is abusive can seriously harm your mental and emotional health. Sometimes, it can even lead to posttraumatic stress disorder (PTSD).

Because of how close family members usually are, you might assume that you are too close for it to be possible for one of them to be toxic.

But the truth is that toxic relationships can happen anywhere with anyone—and family is no exception.

So, what do you do when somebody in your family is toxic?

First, it helps to understand why this person might act this way. If you are aware of their motivations, it is easier to talk to them about their behavior and convince them to change their ways. There are many reasons why somebody might treat you disparagingly:

They are unaware of how their actions affect others. The person does not take into account how their actions and words could make others feel, or worse, they know of the consequences but disregard them and carry on as usual.

They want to look down on other people. Perhaps your family members act this way because they think putting you down will help them feel better about themselves. It might be a sign of low self-esteem or just a mean streak.

They fear abandonment and rejection. Maybe your mom or sister always puts you down because they fear you won't like them if they don't. Maybe your father is constantly angry because he's worried he's not good enough to be part of the family. Sometimes people lash out in anger because they want you to reject them so that they can justify leaving (Logue, 2019).

They feel inferior. Sometimes, somebody is mean because they feel like they are not as good as you. Maybe they don't have a college degree, didn't amount to much in life, or just feel like an outsider in the family. In this case, their actions are driven by their insecurities, and you need to get them to see what they're doing and accept and love them for who they are.

They are scared of losing control. People get manipulative and controlling when something goes wrong or anticipate something bad might happen. In this case, they'll hold on to some things and try to control everything around them. Embracing this is not the same as agreeing with it, but it helps to know where to draw the line.

They are addicted. Sometimes, somebody is acting toxic to escape reality or numb themselves from their problems. They might drink a lot, smoke, or even use substances like marijuana or hard drugs so that they don't feel anything and can ignore bad feelings.

They are acting out of their frustrations. Perhaps the way your family member is acting is a result of a recent event. Perhaps something happened to them that caused them to view other people negatively. Sometimes people act this way towards other people just to vent.

They are sadistic and enjoy hurting others. Some people act this way simply because they enjoy hurting others. This can take place in many ways, but it usually comes out as an angry, mean person who is constantly putting down others to feel better about themselves. But the truth is that a sadistic person is just not a good human being and will never be able to compensate for what they've done by being nicer afterward.

How To Deal with the Consequences of a Dysfunctional Family

The first step after determining whether you come from a dysfunctional family is to admit and recognize the behaviors and habits you have developed due to being raised in a dysfunctional household. You are enduring the consequences of growing up in such a setting as adults. There are numerous methods to handle it, including:

1. Assume accountability.

You have the power, as an adult, to change your situation and establish a stable emotional environment. It's critical to accept accountability for your actions and figure out how to live up to your and your family's standards.

2. Look for help.

Once you become aware of any negative behaviors or habits, you must seek professional assistance—or assistance of any kind—to change them. It can be challenging to deal with low self-confidence, so having family and friends' support is always beneficial.

3. Be imaginative.

Conflicting circumstances can occasionally foster creativity and expressiveness. Communicating with your family and close friends in a healthy manner is essential to overcoming the damaging consequences of a dysfunctional family. Talk about your ideas and ways to mend broken relationships.

4. Develop trust.

It is challenging to grow up in a society when trust in the adults you have observed in your environment is scarce. If you witnessed your parents' mistrust as a youngster, you would likely exhibit the same trait as an adult. Gain the ability to establish trust with your loved ones over time and with patience.

5. Mend fences with your relatives.

Dysfunctional families are emotionally unstable, and as adults, you have the power to create (or mend) a shattered relationship. Try to forgive and help your family in whatever way you can, starting with modest steps.

Regardless of your background, you will always have the chance as an adult to go within, better yourself, and form deep connections with others.

RECOGNIZING UNHEALTHY FAMILY PATTERNS

Families with dysfunctional dynamics have several traits that highlight the unfavorable dynamics and attitudes of the family members. These are the characteristics of a dysfunctional family:

Poor Communication

Members of a dysfunctional family frequently struggle with open communication and other major communication issues. They never talk about problems; they sweep things under the rug. They frequently yell or engage in screaming bouts, which does not foster a conducive atmosphere for discussions. Family members frequently turn to alternative forms of communication since they don't listen to one another.

Absence of Empathy

There is either no empathy or very little empathy in a dysfunctional family, and kids will become self-conscious in the end. There is no such thing as unconditional love, and problems are always dealt with through behavior modifications, even when they are unnecessary if the child has only made a minor error. There is no room for error, which produces a cramped environment and makes kids constantly fear failing.

Easily Addicted

Children who have observed their parents abusing drugs, alcohol, or both often use these substances as adults to cope with life.

Mental Disorders

Children who witness adults around them struggle with mental illnesses and personality problems as they grow up frequently lack coping skills and mature behaviors. Due to a hereditary propensity, they also frequently experience the same diseases.

Managing Behavior

In other cases, parents who overly micromanage their kids' lives and stunt their development also fail to reward excellent behavior. Children who experience this form of control may begin to distrust their skills and develop trust issues.

Perfectionism

Parents frequently end up placing undue pressure on their children to perform, which causes dysfunctional behavior in them. The fear of defeat is sparked, and the kids inevitably become perfectionists as adults.

Criticism

Children raised in dysfunctional households receive continual criticism for their skills—or lack thereof—and are chastised for their deeds. Parents are frequently patronizing, nasty, and condescending, which causes children to feel helpless and lowers their self-esteem.

Insufficient Autonomy and Privacy

In a dysfunctional family, parents may repeatedly breach a child's privacy and smother them to ensure they have no independence when making decisions. They must constantly monitor what the children are doing and lack open communication or regulations.

No Emotional Assistance

Members of a dysfunctional family do not need sympathy or support. There is no designated area where kids can safely constructively express their feelings. Children frequently grow up alone or far from their parents in such circumstances.

Violence and Abuse

In a dysfunctional household, parents could turn to abusing the child. Children from broken homes may exhibit verbal, physical, sexual, or emotional abuse symptoms. Children see this as commonplace and later exhibit the same behavior as adults.

DECIDING TO CUT TIES WITH TOXIC FAMILY MEMBERS

Cutting ties with one parent, sibling, or significant other can be emotionally bruising. Sometimes, it is advised to take a step back and give yourself time and space. This section will offer practical advice to help you decide if it is time for a break from someone in your life who has been toxic or abusive.

The relationship with your family can be a complex one. Sometimes it can be difficult to figure out whether you are a part of the problem or the solution to your family's ongoing conflict. If you find differentiating yourself from negative situations difficult, here are some things to consider when deciding whether cutting ties with toxic family members is the right decision for yourself and those around you:

- Consider the impact of how much time is spent on certain activities: Family functions, annoying relatives, and long phone calls between siblings. These are just some examples of how much time someone spends with their family every day. If you spend a lot of time with your family and don't like most of what is going on, it might be time to change things up.
- Consider the impact that family members have on your life: If you hate spending time with people who don't support and encourage you, are critical, or are toxic in some way, then it might be better to take a step back from those relationships.
- Consider the cost of staying: The more time you spend with toxic people in your life, the more money you will spend on unnecessary things. If this is extremely draining or negative for you, it might be easier to cut off contact with someone when they're not giving anything positive back.
- Consider the value of cutting ties: The less time you spend with certain people, the better your life will become.
- Consider what kind of relationship you want with a family member: Spending time with family members is a huge part of life, but not all family relationships are the same. Spend some time determining the type of relationship you want with each family member and what they may contribute to or take away from it.
- Consider how much contact you have with certain family members: When you cut ties with someone, it is important to remember that it doesn't mean that you can't make up in the future. If you want to fix your relationship, go for it! Remember that you must choose who gets back into your life and on what terms.
- Consider how relevant the other person is to your life: It is important to remember that family is not a necessary part of life. Family members can be helpful in certain circumstances, but they don't have to be. Family members are a big part of life

but aren't everything. The importance of family and the lack of value people place on family members vary.

Reasons why it's difficult for us to distance ourselves from a toxic family member.

I believe we can all agree that no one should be mistreated. So, why do we give our relatives a free pass? Why do we think we should put up with their hurtful behavior?

We don't consider their actions to be abusive. We acknowledge that it hurts, but we downplay it and find reasons. Although it satisfies the requirements, we are hesitant to label it emotional abuse.

Guilt—Family relationships are rife with expectations; we are expected to look after our aged parents, get along with our siblings, celebrate holidays as a family, respect our elders, maintain the peace, and so on. As a result, you could feel guilty or like you are doing something wrong if you deviate from these expectations—cutting off communication with your family is considered the ultimate sin in their eyes. You must understand that you can only fulfill these demands if your family functions normally. If your family is toxic, they are unjust, unreasonable, and hurtful. It is not unethical, cruel, or selfish to safeguard your wellness, and there are instances when separating yourself from toxic individuals is the only option.

Family loyalty—You were undoubtedly taught that family loyalty is a virtue and that you should be unwaveringly faithful to your family no matter what, which primed you to feel guilty. Respect for individuality and your right to have different thoughts and feelings from your family is part of healthy intimacy, as is care for one another. But family members who assert their independence and speak out against abuse are frequently tried to control using their allegiance.

Fear—It makes sense that fear keeps so many of us in unhealthy partnerships. Breaking up with someone is a significant change; no one can predict how it will turn out. Even though what you're doing is bad for you, it is always simpler to keep doing what you've always done. But it doesn't mean you can't face your anxieties and find solutions to any problems. Give yourself patience, kindness, and a network of support.

Love—The fact that you sincerely love your family despite all the suffering and issues they have brought about may be the largest barrier of all. Perhaps you wish to look after them or help them, or perhaps you have warm memories of your previous interactions with them. But as we all know, love alone cannot sustain a relationship, whether it be a friendship, parent-child, or romantic one. Although severing relationships may seem unloving to your family, this does not imply that you no longer care for them. Sometimes, despite our love for someone, we cannot be in a relationship with them.

DEALING WITH AN EMOTIONALLY ABUSIVE/MANIPULATIVE PARENTS

Emotionally abusive or manipulative parents often use guilt and shame to control a child. These tactics make the child feel guilty for questioning the parent and shameful for not obeying him.

As a result, it is hard for children of emotionally abusive or manipulative parents to grow up feeling unloved and insecure about their identities. Some adults may have difficulty defining healthy boundaries or trusting relationships due to these past experiences. It can be worthwhile to talk with others who have been through similar situations to better understand their parents' impact on them and how they are dealing with it now.

Victims of emotional abuse may experience physical and mental health problems due to being made to feel unimportant and unworthy by the abuser. The two people meant to protect us from the world's harsh realities are our parents, but for some of us, that isn't the case (Forray & Yonkers, 2021).

Many of us have emotionally manipulative parents who try to make our lives unpleasant daily. There isn't much assistance available because there isn't much knowledge of the problem. As a result, I have gathered the following list of six strategies for dealing with emotionally abusive parents:

Try to maintain your composure while the abuse is occurring.

No one deserves to be mistreated emotionally, regardless of what they have done, and if it is happening to you, it is wrong. That is the first thing you must remember daily while living in a toxic environment. When you are being abused, it is common to want to lash out, scream, or cry, but try to maintain your composure and resist the urge.

Try to leave the room or take a few long, deep breaths. Hold each inhalation for six seconds before exhaling for three. Remind yourself repeatedly that ignoring this will be in your best interests; keep your distance; and divert your attention to something you find enjoyable, such as picturing yourself on a beach.

Avoid reacting or answering back because doing so will make you feel worse later and negatively affect your mental health, making you uneasy for hours. If what they said has left you feeling too overwhelmed to handle, you can retire to your room and cry, but once you've stopped, try meditation to help you manage your feelings.

Recognize harmful behaviors.

To identify a toxic relationship, you must be able to spot the symptoms of negative behaviors. Some signs of harmful behavior in a family member may include:

- A recurring pattern of insulting and demeaning someone.
- Criticizing another person's opinions or thoughts without compromising any part of one's own.
- Showing disregard for feelings, consent, and individuality by imposing personal views or beliefs on another person.
- Devaluing someone in the pursuit of acquiring power or control over them.

- Using guilt to manipulate their emotional state and actions while keeping their victim unaware that they are being abused cyclically.

The goal is to notice the warning signals and then act to prevent the situations that lead to abuse. You can sit down with your family member and talk about the problem behavior if you have tried to address it with them before but could not come to a resolution.

You must let them know how their behavior is affecting you. If there is no change, it might be time to consider other options, such as seeking outside help or leaving altogether. Although it may seem complex initially, things get much simpler once you get a feel for it.

Try to communicate your feelings.

It is crucial to discuss how emotional abuse affects you since suppressing unpleasant emotions will leave you feeling bottled up, frustrated, and worn out. Later, it may affect both your physical and emotional health.

Your parents' emotional abuse of you might make you feel hopeless, useless, and unworthy. You can express your thoughts to your parents and let them know how their actions make you feel.

You can cite their words, what they have said in a rage, how they have put the blame for everything on you, and how you feel under pressure and can't handle it. Informing your parents and releasing these unpleasant feelings will help you comprehend their relationship. If they don't care, look for other possible solutions.

Discuss it with a senior, a friend, or a qualified person.

While a mentor, friend, or expert may not be able to change your circumstances for you, they can help you cope and maintain your strength. Your top aim should be to feel stronger physically and psychologically, and to do that you must purge all your negative feelings.

These folks will boost your confidence, possibly point out a solution, and—most importantly—help you flush your body's negative emotions to feel better. It can make a difference in your life to receive a text from a friend, a kind word from an elder who compliments you on your strength for handling this, or professional advice on how to handle it.

Never forget that it's acceptable to still love your parents.

Being raised by abusive parents can leave you feeling confused because, let's face it, no matter how they treat you or what they say to you, you still love them. While this is acceptable, loving your parents does not preclude you from discussing what is going on in your life and does not make it wrong to do so.

You can be concerned and show your concern for them, but you should also speak with an adult or a professional, so they can help you and offer you a way out. Your mental health must always come first; never assume for a second that talking to someone outside the home is against your parents.

Spend less time with your parents, if possible.

The first step is always acceptance; after you've acknowledged that your parents are abusive, things may be simple to understand. Spend less time with your parents, if possible. When your parents are abusive, try to avoid being there because staying and paying attention to them can harm your mental health.

You can move out or find other things to do so that you don't spend as much time in the same physical location as your parents. For example, you can spend time away by finding a part-time job, doing chores for your neighbors, staying the night at a friend's house for group study, or volunteering for activities that keep you busy. One of the biggest benefits of moving out and staying out of your parents' way as much as possible, is enjoying life.

It's easy to get caught up in your parents' abusive actions and think it is all part of being a kid: "I'll just do the same thing again and again until they change." But abuse is not normal. It happens because one person decides to dominate another person and uses abuse to achieve their goals, control someone else and put themselves at the top of their hierarchy. If you avoid your parents, you'll never have to deal with them, so enjoying life may be easier.

DEALING WITH EMOTIONALLY ABUSIVE SIBLINGS AND OTHER FAMILY MEMBERS

Dealing with emotionally abusive siblings and other family members can be difficult if you don't know what signs to watch for or how to handle them once you detect them. You might experience a range of emotions that make it hard for you to recognize what is happening. If you suspect someone in your family is emotionally abusing you, here are a few common signs to look for:

Recognize the definition of abuse.

Although there are many different sorts of abuse, it is crucial to comprehend the ideas underlying most of them. Sibling rivalry is frequent, but it becomes abusive when one sibling consistently acts as the aggressor, and the other consistently acts as the victim.

One sibling most frequently commits physical, emotional, or sexual abuse between siblings against the other. Often, abuse is a manifestation of control and power, and it is probably abusive if your sibling tries to make you feel helpless, unappreciated, or unimportant. When in doubt, attempt to get assistance by getting a professional assessment of the circumstances.

Recognize the symptoms of emotional abuse.

Either physical or sexual abuse is supported by emotional abuse, or it might occur alone. An attempt by a sibling to manipulate your ideas and emotions and keep you in a permanent state of fear, shame, or humiliation is known as emotional abuse (Rowntree, 2007). When a sibling is emotionally abused, it can feel like you are constantly on guard since everything you say or do could set them off on a rant or spiral of criticism. Victims of emotional abuse may feel unlovable, unheard, and unimportant.

The continual criticism of your appearance, work, or academic performance by a sibling is one example of the various ways that emotional abuse can manifest. Additionally, it could involve your sibling attempting to persuade you that the rest of your family does not value or care about you.

Look for indications of physical abuse.

Using excessive force or taking other actions to harm another person is known as physical abuse. Physical abuse typically involves using force against another person to exert control over them.

Hitting, kicking, biting, throwing things at another person, or any other physical exertion from an adversary intended to overwhelm a victim are common examples of physical abuse. Some examples of physical abuse symptoms include bruises, fractured bones, burns, bite marks, cuts, abrasions, scars, and other bodily injuries.

Discover the symptoms of sexual abuse.

Any unwanted contact, exposure, or coerced intimate behavior between siblings is sexual abuse, and is frequently the sort of sibling abuse that is least reported and addressed.

It is important to remember that sibling sexual abuse is not about sex (intimacy), but rather about power, control, anger, and frustration. Sibling sexual abuse can occur among preschoolers through adolescents. The incidence rate of sibling sexual abuse is believed to be lower than that of other forms of child sexual abuse, incest, or rape experienced by women and girls (Crabtree, Wilson, & McElvaney, 2021).

However, it is still a serious problem in the lives of many families. Most often, the abuser is male and the abused female, but females can also be abusers. A current study shows that one in 10 boys has been sexually abused by their siblings. This means that some form of sibling sexual abuse has occurred in almost every family at one time or another. Additionally, it could take the form of unwelcome exposure or touching (Rowntree, 2007).

It is best to immediately get in touch with law enforcement or a social worker if you think your home may be a platform for sibling sexual abuse.

Being abused by a relative hurts and may be pretty stressful.

Finding measures to defend oneself is essential, whether the abuse is verbal or physical, such as when someone hits you. You can deal with an abusive relative and move on to more satisfying relationships by talking to your sibling, establishing boundaries, taking time away, and receiving treatment.

Heal From Toxic Sibling Relationship

I could tell you that there are plenty of websites to help you come back from a toxic relationship with your sibling. I could tell you that, in this era of social media, it is easier than ever to stay in touch without being around them. I could even point you towards online forums full of people dealing with this same thing. But what would be the point? You are reading this book because you want some actual advice and insight into how to heal from toxic sibling relationships. So, here are some strategies for handling negative siblings. They are intended to shield you against more harm and perhaps pave the way for developing a wholesome connection.

1. Practice self-care and compassion for yourself.

It's possible for us to feel somewhat compelled to put up with our sibling's mistreatment. After all, they are our family. However, you must begin putting yourself first if you want to recover your well-being and end the cycle of mistreatment.

Use self-compassion and self-care to combat any abuse. Avoid using the words "should" or "must." In other words, consider whether you feel compelled to satisfy your toxic sibling's requirements before letting go of the sense of obligation. Attend to your needs while elevating your sense of value toward a self-governing self.

2. Demonstrate compassion.

Compassion practice is the other half of the self-compassion coin. Even dysfunctional siblings aren't always awful. They may be dealing with difficult personal or professional circumstances, and it's also possible that they haven't learnt how to act in a responsible, healthy manner. They may view the situation very differently from how you do.

Although there is no justification for mistreatment, especially abuse, have you tried to comprehend them? Or did you carry on with the dynamics from your upbringing?

Well, according to C.G. Jung (Modern Man in Search of a Soul), "Until we accept something, we cannot change it. Condemnation oppresses, rather than liberates."

Try to find the strength to forgive them, despite the numerous times you were wounded and betrayed. If nothing else, it is healthy to forgive. That does not mean you should allow your sibling to step on you; it simply entails letting go of the past and not harboring resentment.

3. Reach out.

One of the longest relationships we have is with our siblings. We tend to accept an unhealthy bond as a recurring issue, and we hardly ever ask for aid with such problems. But no matter how long it goes on, seek out if you want to make a change.

Even if you've been mistreated and betrayed repeatedly, try to find the strength to forgive a sibling. If nothing else, forgiving someone is healthy.

You could share your experience with a close family member in a conversation. If you think this is too delicate, talk to a friend who will be sympathetic. One of the most effective instruments for easing the difficulties of distress and trauma is high-quality social support. You become more robust to stress when you have someone to rely on and talk to, maybe through the brain and endocrine processes.

Most importantly, speak with a specialist. To help you break free from the conscious and unconscious bonds and ideas that keep you trapped in unhealthy connections with your sibling, consult a psychologist.

4. Develop assertiveness.

You probably need to practice being assertive if you regularly find yourself getting bullied by toxic siblings.

The hardest relationships to practice assertive communication in are typically those with family members. We don't feel strong enough to establish boundaries since we are too near and exposed, and we have been too accustomed to our relationship's dynamics to alter how we interact. However, it is possible, and your values shouldn't inevitably reflect those of your family and parents.

You are also building a new reality for your connection to develop when you start reprogramming how you communicate with your sibling. You are creating a new version of yourself founded on healthy limits and self-respect. Being assertive implies taking into account both your own and their rights and obligations. Because of this, your toxic siblings will soon understand that they cannot avoid abiding by the new, healthier standards.

5. Let go of the past and your future aspirations.

There is one more thing you must do to alter how you interact with toxic siblings and the effects of your former relationship. It entails letting go of your past. Put the past in the past, and think about a positive future that is joyful and less resentful.

You cannot have a happy future or a prosperous life if you carry the burdens of past mistakes on your shoulders. And you will attract toxic people into your life if you are always looking for someone to hate. It is time to let go of the past, even if you feel it would be good to hold on to it for a few more years.

6. Realize you are not to blame.

It is vital to remember that the abuser is never at fault for the abuse. An abusive sibling may occasionally respond to a discussion, especially if the problem is verbal abuse. Ask if there is a specific cause for your sibling's nasty verbal attacks and express how their insults make you feel.

Jealousy might occasionally arise as kids vie for their parent's attention (these competitive patterns can persist into adulthood). However, you might discover that your sibling's main issue is a sense of inadequacy or alienation.

They can be "taking out" their stress on you and other stressors at school or work. Tell your sibling that while you understand and still care about them, the way they are treating you is not acceptable. If everything else fails, discuss the abuse with a parent or get professional assistance to handle it safely.

7. Establish limits.

Having locks on your doors may assist, but it is only a temporary fix if the violence is physical, and you share a home with the abusive sibling. Speak to a parent or another responsible adult who can help keep you safe from your violent sibling in this situation. Never be scared to contact the police if your safety is in danger.

Setting boundaries is beneficial regardless of whether the abuse is physical or emotional. Physical boundaries are simpler to establish once you have left the home of your family of origin, such as refusing to host an abusive brother at your house or declining invitations to family gatherings.

Refusing to answer calls can be helpful if the abuse is emotional. Even though the sibling may try to annoy you in various ways or by using other family members, you have every right to respond, "The things you say and do are painful." I won't speak to or see you if you keep up with this conduct.

8. Recognize how your abuser thinks.

According to a research journal by Pediatrics, there is a significant risk to other children living in a household where one child is mistreated, most notably a higher chance of fractures and hospitalizations due to abuse. Children are more prone to act out these scenarios later if they witness violence (Rebbe, Sattler, & Mienko, 2022).

And even though not every child in a household will experience abuse, damaged children may become violent towards their siblings. According to a study journal by Child Abuse and Neglect, people who have been molested as young children frequently experience mental health issues even as adults (Forray & Yonkers, 2021).

Talking to your abusive sibling on the phone about your suspicion that they were a victim before turning abusive may be a good idea. Opening a line of communication with compassion, encouragement, and assistance might significantly reduce these behaviors.

To receive help and prevent harm, talk to someone else about this issue, such as a school guidance counselor, if you currently reside with your abusive sibling or are younger than eighteen. Getting professional help for both of you can make it easier for you to deal with an abusive sibling.

9. Undertake therapy.

Given that sibling relationships frequently serve as a model for many of our subsequent relationships, it is worthwhile to work on them, heal from any unhealed past traumas, and capitalize on the existing closeness. It can still be beneficial to process some of the repressed anger, grief, and resentment so that your parents' ghosts don't follow you around. Exercises like sitting in an empty chair or writing a letter you never sent could benefit individual therapy.

Family counseling could be very beneficial if your siblings are open to it. Adult family members can share old tales and pain, end sibling abuse, and change unhealthy sibling relationship dynamics. Sibling family therapy may help all of you accomplish the following:

- Recognize the harmful aspects of your encounters.
- Process the anger and resentment from your upbringing that has been buried.

- Be close without becoming entangled and establish appropriate boundaries that are neither too strict nor too porous.
- Respect one another's uniqueness and create a strong bond where you can assist one another.

Sometimes reaching out to your sibling is the best course of action. And other times, we might need to let go and realize that we don't have the sibling love we desire.

Although we might not be able to influence how our siblings act, we can alter our viewpoints and attitude. We can learn to accept our siblings as they are—flawed yet human, just like ourselves—through in-depth dialogue, shadow work, or with the aid of therapy. They have suffered injuries as well and are doing their best to survive. We can potentially get past previous pain and trauma by realizing our shared humanity, releasing ourselves from the weight of hate and bitterness, and stopping letting the past define who we are for the rest of our lives.

FAMILY TOXIC RELATIONSHIPS WORKSHEET

How to overcome emotional abuse and trauma that come from family relationships.

Are you still holding out some hope that the abusive relationship with your mother/father/sibling will change?

....

....

....

How do you feel about trying to contact your mother/father/sibling if they're willing to work on the relationship?

....

....

....

Do you have any expectations for a relationship with them after recovery?

....

....

....

Are you still holding out some hope of reconciliation with this abusive relative? Why or why not?

....

....

....

Are there any positive things that you can do now to build your self-esteem and build more confidence in yourself?

....

....

....

Are there things you've been doing, such as searching for more information about abuse, joining support groups, etc.?

....

....

....

When you've had enough of a relationship with the abusive person, are you willing to go no contact before cutting off all ties?

....

....

....

Have you ever considered making a phone call to this person? How do you feel about the idea?

....

....

....

Is there anything that would make you want to contact this person(s) again someday?

....

....

....

Do you believe in the power of positive change and growth, or do you feel that things are hopeless for anyone who has suffered abuse or neglect?

....

....

....

6

EXTREME COURSES OF ACTION

When push comes to shove and an abuser still refuses to respect your boundaries or give you a break, it might be time to consider going no contact. This chapter discusses how that works.

FINDING CLOSURE WITH YOUR ABUSER

Giving closure to the abusers would mean admitting that they did something wrong, and they would have to admit that the abuse occurred in the first place. They won't want to fess up to anything that makes them look bad, let alone that.

Some of them might do that; some might realize that they have a problem and genuinely want to work to get better, so they will admit to their wrongdoing. Many won't.

If your relationship is with a narcissistic, sociopathic, or psychopathic abuser, it is almost guaranteed that they won't acknowledge it. True to form, they'll just turn it around on you and gaslight you, as we've already discussed. If you can't even get them to admit there was abuse, you'll never get closure from them.

They also won't want to surrender their power over you, and that is exactly what they would be doing by helping you get closure in your relationship. To give you closure would be to allow you to move on with your life. They would be letting both of you know that they don't have power over you anymore. Again, some of them might realize that they are troubled and will give you this peace, but most of the time doesn't happen.

Instead, you must find closure in yourself. The only way is to focus on yourself, not your abuser, and your recovery. Once I began to truly process my experience and focused on reclaiming my own life rather than longing for some certificate of resolution from my ex, I found that I could finally move on. I could start to be myself again.

HOW TO GO NO-CONTACT WITH A NARCISSIST OR AN ABUSER

A no-contact rule is a strategy for severing ties with narcissists, sociopaths, and other emotional manipulators. As the name implies, it is about cutting all ties with the emotional manipulator and ceasing all communication with them, so that we can no longer interact in any way.

Breaking up with a narcissist is not the same as breaking up with an emotionally healthy person. Leaving a narcissist is a difficult and dangerous process. When someone tries to set boundaries between them or end the relationship, narcissists feel rejected. They can't accept a breakup like a normal person. They will go to any length to keep you, their narcissistic nutritional source.

Many people have questions about the no contact rule, but one common theme is that many victims approach it with the wrong mindset. They see no contact as a form of retaliation. They want to inflict pain on the narcissist. They want them to miss them, regret everything they've done, and return crawling. What happens if you try to break off contact with a narcissist?

They can return to the idealization stage (for a time).

To win you back, they can behave once more like a loving and caring partner. They can tell you how much they adore you and how difficult it is for them to live without you. They can make empty promises and make you nostalgic for the good old days. During this time, you'll probably get some lovely gifts and praises.

Perhaps they are trying to make you feel so terrible.

They can both remind you of your past errors (or what to them appeared to be errors) and the kind things they've done for you (in an exaggerated way). They could accuse you of being excessively egotistical, selfish, and assuming they will always be there for you.

They can use emotional blackmail and slander to their advantage.

They can tell you that no one will believe you, that your word will be worthless compared to theirs, that everyone will see what kind of person you are, that you are nothing without them, that you will be completely alone without them, and so on. They can also begin talking behind your back to ensure that no one believes a word you say.

They can completely discard you.

Even if it's a remote possibility, they may not care about losing you, especially if they are narcissistic. They may argue that you didn't deserve them in the first place or that you were unworthy of them. They may tell others that they were the ones who ended the relationship, or they may begin flaunting about with someone new immediately after ending it with you.

For a no-contact rule to work, you have to be willing and able to do it. If you still have feelings for the narcissist or are in denial about the abuse, they may sabotage your efforts. The sooner you acknowledge what has happened and completely distance yourself from the narcissist, the better.

You don't need proof that you were abused; you know what's happened. You want your boundaries respected and your emotional needs met. You want an emotionally healthy partner who is reliable and honest with you (Thompson, Bonomi, Anderson, Reid, Dimer, Carrell, & Rivara, 2006). You want your relationships to be authentic. You want honesty and transparency in your relationship.

No contact is often used as a form of control by narcissists. They want you to feel powerless and want to control every aspect of your life, including your feelings towards them. Never stop looking for signs that you've been abused, but remember that it is a process, and it takes time for victims to get their abuse out of their system.

CO-PARENTING WITH AN ABUSIVE EX-SPOUSE

When a victim of domestic violence eventually leaves, they do not want to return to that painful and frequently devastating experience. However, if you share children with your abuser, you could feel as though you must keep going through the agony of the abusive relationship even after your divorce. Regardless of domestic violence between parents, co-parenting is frequently mandated. While the motivation behind this is the well-intentioned desire to maintain parental involvement for the welfare of the child, there are some circumstances when this responsibility may put the child at risk of damage or repeated abuse.

What is Co-Parenting?

Co-parenting requires both parents to cooperate amicably and respectfully to provide for the child's needs. Co-parenting is challenging regardless of the background of abuse, but it is considerably more challenging when trying to find areas of agreement with the abuser. With good reason, you might not want to work with your past abuser. Nevertheless, your child is watching and needs the safety and consistency you can give through lawful co-parenting. Children learn vital qualities from successful co-parenting, including patience, compromise, responsibility, and respect. Your child gains the skills needed to thrive through adversity by watching you endure the difficulty and anguish of the abusive past. You also serve as an example of what it means to make sacrifices. Here are some strategies for protecting yourself while honoring your co-parenting commitment in light of this.

SAFE CO-PARENTING WITH YOUR FORMER ABUSER

Recognize your legal rights and represent yourself.

Knowing your legal rights and protections as a parent can help lower your risk of injury if your ex has a history of using manipulation to gain what they want from you or your child. You should bring up these concerns in custody battles if your ex physically abused you or your child. An abuse victim could occasionally be reluctant to express these worries in court for fear that doing so might invite further assault.

To genuinely evaluate what is in the child's best interest, the court needs to be fully informed of the family background. Domestic abuse may affect which parent is awarded primary custody and may result in severe restrictions on the abusive parent's visitation rights. The judge will consider all this information for your child's protection and well-being.

Protection or a restraining order may also be required if you are concerned that your abuser will hurt you again.

Set up clear channels of communication and boundaries.

The most caring, sensible, or reasonable people are not abusive people. Your ex will likely try to twist your comments and control events to make it appear as though you are the more responsible parent than they are, or even try to make your child hate you. The fact that you must co-parent with your abuser does not require you to continue to put up with their mistreatment or manipulation. You should establish clear boundaries and be aware of your limits. This needs some planning and consideration, but it is worthwhile.

You can't rely on things to resolve themselves or on your initiative to figure things out in the end. These restrictions must be understood and established upfront. Hours of communication, methods of communication, and specific directions on how to communicate with the child while in the other parent's care are all crucial boundaries.

For instance, it could be necessary to let your ex know in writing that they cannot contact or email after 8 pm if you know you put your child to bed at 8 pm and are sleeping by 9 pm. Setting explicit parameters for the number and timing of calls or FaceTimes your co-parent can have with your child regularly will uphold your authority and stop the harassment.

Establishing a communication strategy using planning tools is another way to avoid harm or manipulation when co-parenting with an abuser. Co-parents can plan activities, establish custody schedules, and talk about child-related issues using scheduling tools in a system impervious to manipulation or change. Conversations over the phone can quickly get heated, leading to "he said/she said" arguments. Emails are more secure, but they can still be changed or removed. A more trustworthy and accountable form of communication is a scheduling app.

Have a self-executing custody agreement

It would be fantastic if you could draft a separation agreement that specifies the conditions of legal and physical custody in a way that equitably expresses the preferences of both parents while advancing the child's best interests. You should include a precise and unambiguous custody schedule in this agreement.

The last thing you desire to have in a co-parenting arrangement with a controlling ex is any room for ambiguity that can give them more leverage over you or the circumstances. For instance, if you plan to divide Christmas Eve and Christmas Day, the agreement should include precise pick-up or drop-off and return hours. This can assist in stopping the abuser from exploiting the child as a means of controlling or denying you parental rights by claiming a misunderstanding or breakdown in the communication that took place.

Alternatively, your specific custody arrangements can be determined through a consent court order if you and your ex cannot reach a separation agreement. Whatever the legal procedure used to obtain the agreement, you should insist that it be concise, specific, and self-executing.

Maintain safe areas and defend yourself.

All in-person interactions should take place in a secure public area for your protection and your child's protection. The school or daycare where your child attends would make a good setting. You might also wish to invite a neutral party, which would give you additional stability and support while also easing the strain.

Report violations and attempt to maintain composure.

An abusive ex is likely to break the separation agreement or custody arrangement. Suppose your ex frequently picks up or returns the child beyond the scheduled time, keeps the child overnight when it has been forbidden, or plans activities with your child that take place during your custody time.

In that case, they are not following the provisions of your custody agreement. You should maintain your composure and avoid directly confronting your ex in these situations. It could be wise to begin by having your lawyer send a letter to your ex demanding that they uphold their share of the child custody arrangement. If this doesn't work, you can file a motion of contempt, ask the judge to make adjustments, or request mediation.

Co-parenting is not simple, and the challenges become much more complicated when your ex seriously injures your physical or emotional well-being. It may be difficult, although it's not impossible to co-parent safely with an abuser. These pointers are meant to assist you as you navigate this difficult period. Support is one of the vital things a past abuse victim requires. You are not alone in this, and by establishing sensible limits, you can protect your safety and well-being while letting your kids continue to live with the other parent.

PLAN A SAFETY STRATEGY

Safety plans are a series of measures that can reduce your chances of suffering harm at the hands of your partner or abuser. It contains details about you and your life that are particular to you and will improve your safety at home, school, and other locations.

This safety planning tool has several sections, so take your time and read through them. In order to assist you in determining your safety alternatives, a series of questions will be asked of you. You can use this tool alone, with a friend, or with a trusted adult.

REMEMBER: The information you provide must be truthful and accurate for this safety plan to be effective for you.

EXTREME COURSE OF ACTION WORKSHEET

When push comes to shove and an abuser still refuses to respect your boundaries or give you a break, then it might be time to consider going no contact

When did it become clear to you that you have to go no-contact?

....

....

....

What's your biggest fear about completely cutting off ties with this relationship?

....

....

....

What is it about this relationship that scares you the most?

....

....

....

If you were to be completely honest with yourself, how would you define fear?

....

....

....

Do you feel like there's something missing in your relationship once you're gone, or do you feel that things will go back to normal after a while?

....

....

....

Is there anything in your life right now that reminds you of this person or their actions towards you?

....

....

....

Have you ever been tempted to contact the other party(s). How do you feel about this temptation?

....

....

....

Do you believe there's any hope of salvaging this relationship?

....

....

....

What evidence could support that belief?

....

....

....

7

WATCH OUT FOR VICTIM SYNDROME

In the aftermath of emotional abuse, it is possible to develop victim syndrome. This chapter explains how to avoid this toxic trap. It is not uncommon to feel like a victim of abuse during and after the trauma. Trauma feels like a violation, so it stands to reason that trauma victims would believe themselves violated.

Most people who experience some form of abuse will develop negative beliefs about themselves, other people, and the world. In most cases, these beliefs are temporary and disappear a few months after the trauma. However, some people have a harder time recovering from trauma and develop victim syndrome, an extreme form of negative beliefs that develop in the aftermath of trauma.

Victim syndrome (also known as victim mentality) is described in pop psychology as "the belief that you are helpless in changing your life and feel like a victim to outside forces" (Wikipedia). This definition is incomplete because it doesn't explain why people develop victim syndrome and what can be done about it. It's also not always accurate because it makes victim syndrome sound like a disorder or mental illness.

WHAT IS A VICTIM MENTALITY/SYNDROME?

Fear, powerlessness, and a victim mentality are so common in relationships. A victim mentality is when someone feels like they are constantly being mistreated and taken advantage of by their significant other. The result is that they have low self-worth and believe their life is not worth living or worth fighting for because they feel like they have no control over their situation.

This syndrome can lead to dangerous consequences such as staying stuck in an unhealthy relationship, self-harm, addiction to alcohol or drugs, or even suicide. One of the ways to overcome this syndrome is through exercising your power and regaining control over your life.

How to Overcome a Victim Mentality/Syndrome

There are many different ways to exercise your power, but it is important to have a goal for the end of this process. If you are in an unhealthy relationship, do not try to live in the relationship like it is always going to get better magically. It probably will not, and you will lose yourself and hope for the best. Get out of the relationship and start feeling whole again. You deserve happiness!

The following tips can help you gain control over your life:

Know who you are. Know what is important to you, who you are, and what makes you happy. Many people with a victim mentality suffer from low self-esteem or lack of identity, making it harder to exercise power over their own lives.

Take care of yourself. Start taking care of your body and mind. Eat healthy, exercise, meditate, read positive and uplifting books, spend time with family and friends and live a more fulfilling life. Some people suffer from mental illnesses that make exercising power harder for them to do, so seek help first if this is a problem area for you.

Turn your life around. Have you ever heard the phrase, "Don't wait for someone to save you. You have to save yourself"? Well, it is brutally honest and so true! You do not have to stay in a bad situation. Begin thinking of things that make you happy that aren't drugs or unhealthy relationships, and force yourself to get out there and do those things. Create a new life for yourself. You'll be amazed at how much happier you will be.

Date healthier people. You deserve happiness! Find someone who treats you well and cares about your feelings and your own. Don't settle for someone who is emotionally or physically abusive just because they are nice sometimes or give you attention. They are not worth your time or love if they display abusive patterns. Find someone who treats you how you want and deserve to be treated, and date them. Recall that it can be very helpful for a victim to take some personal time to heal and get to know themselves better first, before dating or starting a relationship again.

Learn from it. It is very easy to get into a victim mentality when you have been hurt in the past. However, if you do not learn from those experiences and let them go, you will most likely fall for that same thing again because you did not learn the lesson that was trying to be taught to you. Take what happened, learn from it, and make yourself a better person due to these experiences.

Fake it until you make it. Yes, it sounds silly and kind of stereotypical, but many people in a victim mentality do not know how to exercise power in their own lives. They think that they cannot or should not do things on their own or that they should always wait for someone to come to save them. You have to learn how to take control of your life and choose healthy relationships for yourself. It is hard, but if you try, you will at least feel on a level playing field with everyone else.

Practice self-love and respect. If you do not love yourself, how can you expect anyone else to? It is important to respect yourself and your feelings to have healthier relationships in the future.

When you fall for a victim mentality, it can be hard to get out of because it becomes your identity. You start seeing yourself as the "victim," which impacts every single relationship you are in. People usually try to break away from this pattern by themselves without any counseling or therapy, but it can be very hard to do. If you are stuck in a victim syndrome or are afraid that you are heading down that path, then find help now. Counseling and therapy can help you learn how to get out of the victim syndrome and embrace a more fulfilling life.

SIGNS THAT YOU HAVE VICTIM SYNDROME

Do you feel like it is impossible to get out of your current situation? Do you have no hope for the future because you feel like everyone has a better life than you do? Are you willing to put up with bad behavior from others just so they will stay in your life? If the answer is correct, you may suffer from victim syndrome.

You may wonder why someone would put themselves in these situations, and I agree with these feelings. However, I also believe that sometimes people cannot see their worth and value when they get stuck in this thinking pattern. These people feel trapped and helpless no matter what happens, so they stay in unhealthy relationships or situations for fear of being alone or dying alone.

Below are signs you have victim syndrome:

- You blame yourself for everything that is going wrong in your life.
- You do not believe you are worthy of having happiness in your life.
- You believe that everyone, including your family and friends, has a better life than you.
- All your relationships feel like a living nightmare, and you've tried everything to escape this situation, but it just keeps getting worse.
- You constantly think about ending it all and dying because it feels more "real" than what is happening in the present moment.
- You feel like a victim in every relationship where you are involved.

- You feel you do not deserve to be happy, and it is impossible to change your life for the better because you will never be enough for a happy ending.

There are many reasons people develop victim syndrome, but most of the time, it is from their trauma or abuse in childhood or adolescence. This can happen when family members try to control your life and what happens in your home. It can also happen when a person believes their parents rejected them when they were young because they did not give them enough support or direction when they were growing up.

This doesn't mean you must accept blame and responsibility. Try responding with empathy.

It is challenging for people to get out of the victim mentality when they are in unhealthy relationships because it makes them feel like there is no way out. They do not want to leave their relationship, but they also do not want to stay in the vacuum they feel when they are alone (Staff, 2022). They may stay and hope that things will eventually improve, but this will most likely only lead to a worse situation and never an improvement.

THE VICTIM, VICTIMIZER, AND RESCUER CYCLE

In the 1960s, Stephen Karpman offered the first explanation of the Drama Triangle. It illustrates a power game with three roles: victim, rescuer, and persecutor. Each position symbolizes a typical and unproductive way of dealing with conflict (Remschmidt, 2011). One can take the trip around the triangle alone or with someone else, such as a partner, child, coworker, etc. Most of us are neurologically wired to play one of these three roles, and depending on the situation, we may do so consciously or unconsciously.

The Victim

The victim's role is the one most people are wired to play. When someone is in the victim position, they feel powerless to control outcomes, and their responses to stress may be unpredictable and extreme. Victims may perceive themselves as weak, powerless, or helpless. They also tend to think that other people's actions are aggressive and threatening rather than seeing them as out of alignment with their needs. In any situation that is power imbalanced, the victim will likely experience a loss of personal boundaries.

Victims often feel oppressed, confined, helpless, and sad. They believe that life is out of their control. They don't believe they can alter their lives, and they are hesitant to accept responsibility for their unfortunate situations.

Victims believe they are helpless or incapable and place the blame on the persecutors (it can be other people or a particular situation). They always look for rescuers to take care of their problems. The victims won't be able to make decisions, deal with difficulties, alter the situation, or have any sense of satisfaction or accomplishment if they remain in the "dejected" attitude.

The Rescuers

The Rescuers play an important role in any relationship where there is a power imbalance; however, such relationships do not often last long-term because rescuers cannot solve problems alone. In a relationship, the rescuer may be an adult child, wife, or parent. In this role, they feel obligated to help others in need and often feel like they are the only ones who can help. Rescue roles can appear similar to victim roles as they both involve a loss of personal boundaries. Rescuers tend to deny their feelings and needs while attempting to rescue others; however, this denial may lead them to take on an angry or judgmental stance toward others when they don't get their way.

The Persecutors

The Persecutors use power in an unbalanced manner through verbal or physical assaults on others and are conscious of the imbalance of power in any situation. Persecutors often feel threatened by others, which can lead them to become aggressive and defensive. Persecutors have little regard for boundaries and often plan out every move to ensure that they feel safe. Like the rescuer, the persecutor plays an important role when there is a power imbalance in a relationship.

Persecutors temper their behavior by taking into account the welfare of their victims; however, they still maintain an unequal power relationship with their victims. Attackers are similar to "Critical Parents," who are tough, firm, and establish boundaries. They frequently believe that they must prevail at all costs.

Without offering the necessary direction, support, or a resolution to the issue, the persecutors place the responsibility on the victims and criticize the behavior of the rescuers. They control with order and rigor and are critical and skilled at detecting faults. They maintain victimization and occasionally exhibit bullying behavior.

Are you a persecutor, a rescuer, or a victim?

You are now familiar with the Drama Triangle and its roles. Which do you identify with—victim, rescuer, or persecutor?

If you are human, you'll likely encounter situations when you perceive all three as you or how others perceive you. It is vital to note that during a mind game, the participants in the Drama Triangle may exchange roles, and if one role in the triangle changes, the other two roles also shift.

When you have your life under control, you can take care of yourself and live a full life.

The victim mentality causes us to believe that we are weak and powerless, so we need others around us to rescue us from our problems. Rescuers always perceive the problem as the victim's fault and their need to fix it. The persecutor sees others as an enemy to conquer.

You must take charge of your life if you want to escape the victim's attitude. Be willing to take responsibility for yourself and your actions. You must use boundaries in your life because if you don't, everyone will walk all over you. Use your power for good! If someone is treating you poorly, then stop being friends with them. Love yourself enough not to tolerate being treated badly by others, regardless of how much you think they love or care about you. For many people, the victim mentality is a myth (or false belief) that they believe about themselves, but it is not true.

SELF-PITY AFTER EMOTIONAL ABUSE AND TRAUMA

Fighting self-pity can be difficult when you've recently experienced emotional abuse or trauma. In cases like these, it may feel impossible to move on and start healing. Following the painful feelings, there are actions you may take to enhance your life and advance.

The first step is acceptance. Accepting what has happened will help you put things into perspective and give you peace of mind. You might have a different way of expressing your emotions now than before the event; this doesn't mean that your emotional responses have changed, just that they may be different from the typical responses.

Another way you can deal with self-pity is by **getting some professional help**. A professional counselor or therapist can guide you through the rough experience and help you to recover more quickly. If neither the self-help nor support from others helps, consider speaking with a medical doctor. Sometimes, prescription medications can be very helpful in dealing with intense emotions like self-pity.

Keep in mind that recovery doesn't happen overnight. Allow yourself time to heal, and make sure to give it an appropriate amount of time—don't rush yourself into recovery, as this will only leave you feeling incomplete and frustrated. You can start to feel better when you accept what happened and let go of self-pity.

Self-pity is an emotion that occurs when one has a negative view of oneself, which can be triggered by occurrences inside or outside of your control. It is a good idea to pause when you feel horrible about yourself and consider what you might have done better to avert the circumstance that caused your poor feelings.

Do not be scared to seek expert assistance if all else fails. It is hard to recover from emotional abuse or trauma, but with the right tools and support in place, you will benefit greatly in the future. Follow these tips and focus on getting over self-pity.

Emotional Abuse's Short-Term Effects Include:

- Solitude
- Low self-esteem
- Shame and fear in social situations
- Avoiding related activities Feeling powerless

Emotional Abuse's Long-Term Effects Include:

- Disorders
- Neuroticism, or low mood, negative emotions, or chronic stress
- Body aches and heart palpitations are health issues
- Relationship issues
- Emotional apathy
- Child emotional abuse effects

Emotional Abuse Can Have These Effects on Children:

- Changed behavior. Children may "act out," have ADHD, or be abusive to other kids.
- Child emotional abuse can cause self-harm and suicidal thoughts.
- Development emotionally. Emotionally abused children may have trouble managing their emotions. Abuse may make them less emotionally mature than their peers, as it hinders their ability to trust their emotions.
- Misbehaving. A 2014 research study shows how childhood emotional abuse can lead to unhelpful coping in women (Calvete, 2014). It can cause numbing or emotional disconnection. Other kids may turn to fantasy, leading to avoidance and isolation.

Victims of crime and other unfortunate events often develop a victim mindset. They feel that things are always happening to them, that others are always responsible for their misfortune, and that they can do nothing to prevent or change things. If you find yourself developing a victim mindset, it's important to be aware of the risk factors so you can take steps to counter them.

If you want to be powerful in your life, learn how to use your power each day by creating an empowering mindset that allows you to live life on your terms!

VICTIM SYNDROME WORKSHEET

The questions below are designed to help you identify if you are suffering from victim syndrome and if so, the steps that can be made to change it.

YES OR NO ANSWERS NEEDED

Have I been blaming myself for something that happened that was not my fault?

Do I still blame myself after accepting what happened?

Do I have a feeling of hopelessness about my situation?

Do I take what comes my way as a personal attack against me?

Is there any way that I am taking responsibility for conditions in my life?

If yes, how bad is the feeling of terror that accompanies the thought of returning to the old situation? In detail...

....

....

....

What signs of victim syndrome are already present in your life?

....

....

....

Do you feel sorry for yourself and feel helpless about recovering from your abuse?

....

....

....

Can you identify the three basic elements of victim syndrome: identifying with the aggressor, self-pity/depression, and blaming others?

....

....

....

Have you been able to eradicate them from your life?

....

....

....

Is it right for an abuse victim to seek forgiveness and reconciliation with his/her abuser, if he/she is truly sorry for their actions?

....

....

....

Why is this important in healing from abuse?

....

....

....

How can this be accomplished effectively without enabling the abuser or making you feel like a doormat for them?

....

....

....

8

TAKING CARE OF YOURSELF BIG-TIME

It can be challenging to take care of yourself, especially when you cannot find the right words to say or do. It is easy to feel devastated and helpless during these moments. In this chapter, I'll give you some tips on how to take care of yourself big-time and remember your purpose while giving yourself the best chance of success.

SELF-COMPASSION AND EMPATHY ARE IMPORTANT

Treating oneself with the same understanding you would for a loved one at times of failure or adversity is known as self-compassion. It enables us to accept or work through our shortcomings while also being compassionate to ourselves as we do so.

Self-care is the exercise of looking after your mind, body, and spirit by partaking in stress-relieving and well-being-promoting activities. It is a nudge to you and others that your needs come first. Everyone has a right to good relationships with others and healthy relationships with oneself. Whether romantic or not, we all deserve to be treated with dignity, trust, and respect.

And as with any relationship, you should make sure you, too, are treating yourself well. You should always be your ally. After all, you must look out for yourself before anyone else can do so for you.

Practicing self-care regularly is the greatest opportunity to maintain a healthy level of mental health. Self-care can be as simple as choosing what to eat or when and where you eat it. As critical as it is to sustain a healthy diet, it's also necessary to maintain good hygiene and take care of our physical appearance. This includes our skin, hair, and nails.

Taking care of your physical appearance is the first step to a healthy lifestyle, and being healthy physically benefits your mental health as well. Knowing that you have a clean body and proper hygiene practices will lower stress levels and help prevent panic attacks, depression, and other mental illnesses. It can also enhance your sleep habits and overall quality of life.

Taking care of yourself starts with taking care of your health. However, self-care is certainly not just about taking medicine but also respecting ourselves in all aspects of our lives, including our minds and bodies.

Along with setting boundaries, creating a solid support system, and taking care of yourself comes the ability to be compassionate and empathetic to yourself. Often, we're so wrapped up in things we say or do that we forget about the bigger picture—why are we doing this?

AVOID NEGATIVE THOUGHT PATTERNS

When we are distracted from our purpose, it is very easy to lose sight of what is important. If you feel like you don't have a purpose right now or you've hit a wall on your purpose, please be sure to check out the below.

Think About Your Self-Care Routine

Self-care is a significant part of staying healthy and happy. Whether in therapy, meditation, physical exercise, or anything else, these practices allow you to be receptive to new ideas and have the opportunity to reflect on what you've learned.

It's okay to need time after a hard day to decompress and not think about anything. When we fail to give ourselves the chance to recover, it could hinder our ability to jump into something new.

Look for What You Can Accomplish

Think about what your purpose is now and what goals you want to accomplish. Redefining yourself—not just getting a fresh start—is important when it comes down to finding the next step in your life story.

Make a Plan

It is easy to let go of things when you're exhausted and under stress, but it is important to make a plan of action for the next few days. For example, if you are in therapy, consider finding a time to talk with your therapist over the phone, so that you can have more open lines of communication.

Be Willing to Change Your Habits as Needed

We all have these bad habits that cause us emotional overwhelm. Breaking bad habits is incredibly difficult sometimes—especially when we are tired or stressed. However, we must challenge ourselves to break new habits—not just because it's good for us, but because these actions can help you achieve your purpose faster.

Choose Your Friends Wisely

It is important to surround yourself with people who inspire you and whose energy is contagious. Think about your friends and if they are pushing you in the right direction or offering support when you need it. You can also look at your current relationships and see if anything toxic or hurtful is going on.

Be Present in Every Moment

Sometimes, our thoughts can stray, and we can become mired in the past, the future, or somewhere else. As I have said before, it is easy to confuse your thoughts for your feelings—especially when we're excited—but it is so important to be present in every moment, especially if you want to accomplish something new.

SELF-CARE TIPS TOWARDS RECOVERY FROM ABUSE

When someone who has been emotionally abused gets out of a toxic relationship, their healing journey has just begun. These victims will still experience trauma symptoms like feeling worthless, depression, dissociation, anxiety, nightmares, and recurring flashbacks (Lamoreux, 2021). They could also feel like they need to reconnect or check in with their abuser because of trauma bonds created during the abuse.

Getting help from a therapist specializing in trauma abuse and learning some self-care practices are great ways to learn how to tend to your spirit, body, and mind.

Not every healing method is going to work for everyone, so you need to experiment with the following to find the ones that work best for your journey. These can be very beneficial for your healing, and these practices have the potential to save your life on your journey to recovery:

Exercise

Having a daily exercise routine could save your life. Find something that you enjoy doing and do it daily. It could be swimming, running, walking, dancing, or whatever; just get up and move. If you don't have a lot of motivation, begin small. Start by committing to 15 minutes of walking instead of running. When you exercise, it lowers cortisol levels and releases endorphins. It replaces the addictions we developed with our abuse and gives us a better outlet.

Exercise lets you embody your strength and resilience after you leave your abuser. It can help you battle the biochemical addiction your body developed during the abuse.

Serotonin, adrenaline, cortisol, and dopamine are a few substances that contribute to this addiction by amplifying the relationship with the abuser during the highs and lows of the abuse. Exercise can start countering the side effects of the abuse, like illness, sleeping disorders, premature aging, and weight gain caused by our immune system being overwhelmed by trauma.

Sleep

Being well-rested is essential for your mental well-being. Depression, anxiety, stress, and trauma can affect people's sleep patterns. Sometimes it gives them nightmares, and they can't fall asleep at night. Still, other times, they can't manage to stay awake. At the same time, not getting enough sleep can also make depression, anxiety, stress, and trauma even worse, creating a vicious cycle that will only send you into a downward spiral.

You must ensure you get enough sleep, normally 7 to 9 hours a night, depending on the individual. Get to bed almost the same time every night and set the alarm to get up at the same time every morning. If you encounter any difficulties with sleeping, talk to your primary care physician.

Meditation

When you have been traumatized, the areas in the brain that are related to functioning, such as focus, regulating emotions, planning, memory, and learning, get disrupted. Meditation has been proven to help certain areas of the brain, like the hippocampus, amygdala, and prefrontal cortex.

Mediation puts the survivor back into the driver's seat, giving them the ability to heal their brain and reclaim their reality from empowerment instead of trauma.

Daily meditation can strengthen neural pathways positively. It can lead to an increase in grey matter in the brain that relates to regulating emotions and diminishes the flight-or-fight response that goes a bit crazy during trauma (Logue, 2019). Meditation makes you more aware of your cravings to have contact with your abuser and allows you to be more mindful of your emotions. This gives you space to think about alternatives before you act impulsively and return to the toxic relationship.

Anchoring

Emotional abuse survivors have usually been gaslighted into believing the abuse wasn't real. You need to anchor yourself back to reality instead of idealizing the relationship. This is helpful for survivors when they start to question how real the abuse was, or if they have mixed emotions about their abusers who only show affection just to keep them in the abusive relationship. Most victims have positive emotions toward their abusers because of techniques such as intermittent reinforcement and love bombing. Other survivors might associate them with survival if the abuse threatened their physical and emotional safety.

Anchoring helps you reconnect to the reality that the abuser tried to destroy. It gives the survivor validation and reduces cognitive discord about the true identity of the abuser.

Survivors are very vulnerable once they leave the toxic relationship. The abuser will try to trick them into coming back by putting on their false albeit sweet persona. This is why it is essential to block all phone calls and text messages from your abuser (Lamoreux, 2021). You also have to get rid of all your connections with them and their enablers on all social media. This will get rid of all information and temptation about them. It gives the survivor a clean slate where they can reconnect to the truth about what happened and how they felt instead of how the abuser distorts the situation.

To start anchoring yourself, list the 10 worst incidents during the relationship or 10 ways the abuser made you feel degraded. This will be useful when you get tempted to reach out to them, respond to an attempt to get you back, or look them up.

It would be best to work with a therapist to make this list so you can get help with any triggers that might come up when trying to anchor yourself. If there are incidents that you find triggering, it might be best to pick ones that aren't as triggering until you can manage your emotions in healthy ways.

If you can learn to make statements like "My abuser disrespected me daily" or "They made me feel small each time I succeeded," it can help you remember if you start rationalizing, denying, or minimizing the abuse. It can be difficult to redirect your focus to all the abuse within the relationship, but it can help reduce cognitive discord about the abuser. Reducing cognitive discord is necessary for your recovery.

Yoga

If you are feeling the effects of the trauma in your body, it would be great to use an activity that combines physical activity and mindfulness to help bring empowerment and restore balance. Yoga can help ease anxiety and depression, improve symptoms of PTSD, bolster self-esteem, expand emotional regulation skills, and improve body image.

Yoga lets abuse survivors counter the powerlessness they feel from the trauma stored in the body by engaging in powerful movements. Yoga can provide self-mastery that helps you regain ownership of your body. It lets survivors rebuild their sense of safety that trauma takes away from them. It can also eliminate the feeling of disassociation by reconnecting them to their body.

Creative Pursuits

Creativity is a great outlet for trauma and can have a very soothing effect overall. Creative pursuits allow abuse survivors to express those emotions they have had to suppress for so long and control and manipulate them in ways that they lost the ability to when they entered the relationship with their abuser. Sometimes it's even an activity that they used to enjoy but that the abuser belittled or told them they were no good at, and picking it up again will be symbolic of taking back the life that the abuser had ripped away from them.

It doesn't matter which creative pursuit you prefer—music, art, writing, dance, making collages, and so forth—or even if you're any good at it. As long as you enjoy it, it will help you connect with your emotions and inner self. Additionally, completing a creative project will give you a sense of accomplishment that will raise your self-esteem, even if nobody else will ever see it. If you find out that you also have a knack for it, that will be a happy bonus.

Talk With a Counselor

In dealing with my abusive ex, I mostly visited counselors as a way to leave a record of the abuse to help me get out. When it came to my emotional struggles during the relationship, and after I left him, I turned to a psychiatrist. However, I've spoken with many women who've found that just talking with a counselor has done wonders for them.

I must emphasize here that a counselor will not give you prescriptions for any medication. Psychiatrists can be medical doctors, but mental health counselors are not licensed. If you would like to talk to an impartial third party and get the tools to help you progress and heal from your situation, then counseling or psychotherapy might be able to help you. Finding a counselor could be helpful if you have found those around you either having a hard time accepting the truth about your abuse or are unwilling to help you through it. It is a bitter reality, but it can happen, and when it does, it is nice to have someone to turn to.

Write a Letter to Your Younger Self

Just like acknowledging the abuse is crucial to recovering, being able to forgive yourself for it happening in the first place is crucial for reclaiming your life. When you look back on the abuse, you might be mad at yourself. You might think that all the signs were there, that you were too passive and therefore allowed yourself to be abused. But you have to remember that hindsight is 20/20. Everything seems obvious when you look back on it later.

You need not be mad at yourself because this happened. More than that, you need to forgive yourself for it happening. Otherwise, you'll never be able to reclaim your life. It's like when you are mad at a friend at can't start talking to them again until you talk through things and one or both of you apologize. You need to talk things out with your younger self and forgive yourself.

To this end, write a letter to your younger self. Talk about everything that has taken place since the abuse began. It will be painful, but try to get through it in one sitting if you can. Just let it all out: the frustration, the belittlement, the isolation, the hurt. Then talk about where you're going from here and how things will be better now.

Most importantly, remind yourself that this wasn't your fault and say that you forgive yourself for not being able to stop it sooner. Read this last part out loud if you have to. You might feel stupid doing this at first, but after you've been at it for a while, you'll get more and more into it emotionally and mentally. By the end, you might not fully be at peace with yourself, but at least you'll finally realize that even though the signs were there does not mean you could have done anything. You can finally accept this was not your fault and start to reclaim the life you had before the abuse.

Working With the Inner Child

Even though you were traumatized by an abuser, there might have been other traumas brought about by the relationship. You might have a wounded inner child that needs to be helped by your adult self when you feel emotional. Experience aggravated unmet childhood needs; self-compassion is needed during your healing journey.

Survivors often struggle with self-blame and toxic shame after being abused. They know logically that they had no control over the abuse, but the abuse can bring up old wounds that never healed. It can cause a bigger pattern of always feeling like they are never good enough. Changing how you talk to yourself is critical when healing, and it tackles old narratives cemented in the brain.

Being gentle with yourself is crucial after abuse. The most powerful type of compassion is self-compassion.

If these deep-seated, ancient emotions come up, try to soothe yourself just like you were talking to somebody you truly love. Write some positive affirmations down that you can say to yourself when you are grieving, like: "I am worthy of affection, respect, and love," or "I deserve peace." This will help you learn to exhibit understanding and sensitivity to yourself that curbs self-blame and self-judgment. Self-compassion extends to keeping no contact, too.

When you blame and judge yourself, you will engage in self-sabotage since you don't think you are worthy of joy, stability, and peace. Once you accept that you are going to show compassion toward yourself, you need to remind yourself that you deserve kindness and care.

There is an empowering and victorious life in front of you after abuse. You can thrive and survive, but you have to commit to self-care.

SUICIDE PREVENTION

It's not a comfortable topic, but it is a necessary one. Emotional abuse can reach the point where the victim might contemplate suicide. Even after leaving your abuser, you might reach a low point in your life before your recovery begins. If this happens, don't be afraid to reach out. Talk to loved ones who aren't involved with your abuser—or, at least, who you know won't tell your abuser about any of this. Talk to your primary care therapist or physician. If you feel these thoughts are bearing down on you, call your local suicide prevention hotline number as soon as possible. You will get over this because you are stronger than your abuser has made you out to be.

MAINTAIN SUCCESS ON A PERSONAL LEVEL

The most important part of an abusive relationship might be the first moment within it—the first contact you make with your abuser. This first contact you make may be the most important part of that relationship. How we make first contact with a person and how an abuser makes first contact with a person are massively different, and this shows most of all when we first meet them. The first stage of that relationship is led by that first touch, the first impressions of both parties.

As a victim, when we meet someone, we think about what they are thinking and what that might lead to. As people who tend to live in fear and anxiety for most of our lives after being in the cycle of abuse, we look for a way to escape from almost everywhere we find ourselves. When we're trained as people to be afraid of our partners, we don't have positive experiences with other people, which would assure us to act more calmly.

However, we look at new people we meet as just that—as normal people, more or less. Normal people grow up meeting new people by spending time around them and checking for themselves if they get a good feeling from that person. This is how we are used to interacting with people, and we treat most other people we meet like non-threatening presences. We understand the world around us as relatively safe, and we connect with people out of a desire for security and companionship. We check if their "vibe" is one that we connect with.

Most normal people have a sense of character and can read people for their true characters easily. Some people are better judges of character than others, but most normal people have in common that they spend their time understanding someone better simply through practice. Spending time with someone you know better is the fastest way to get to know them more personally. It is through this repeated interaction that we become closer to other people. That interaction forges a new relationship with them over time, and we get to know them even better. This is the cycle for most normal people, socially.

Abusers, on the other hand, very rarely act this way when they first meet someone. When an abuser first meets someone, they try to sniff out the weaknesses of other people. They see a person as someone who could act as a stepping stone or another pawn to get where they think they need to go. They use everyone they meet if they think there's something in it for them, which mainly includes potential victims for a relationship. When you first meet them, they'll analyze you to try to find out how you function. Abusers usually do not understand how people function, so they focus on understanding people they meet on the most literal level.

This is where abusers locate empaths, in particular—highly sensitive people are usually able to be picked out of a crowd, especially by manipulative people and abusers. Empaths are usually very reactive to meeting new people and will show their emotions on their faces very plainly. They react expressively to other people's feelings, and the abuser understands this and uses it to their advantage by trying to draw emotional responses out of them (Logue, 2019). When they do so, they confirm that they are meeting someone very empathetic, likely to try to sympathize with them whenever they can. In addition, the abuser will try to see if they can gauge how submissive you are when the two of you first meet.

Spending more time with them will offer you more opportunities to defer to them and let them do what they want instead of offering you that opportunity. The more you allow them to exert their will over you at these opportunities, the more the abuser is assured that they can do so farther into the relationship. This entire set of first meetings between the abuser and their victim is the set-up for abuse. They groom their victims, trying to scope out what part of their personality they can take advantage of and to what degree.

When they come into contact with a new person, they immediately begin to look at that person as either someone expendable to their grand plan or someone who they need to keep around for at least the time being. Those who they do keep around are the victims who are often the most empathetic, the most kind to them, the most willing and able to see the good in people and the good in bad people, in particular. Seeing this potential for good things in all people is good and kind, no matter their past actions.

However, not being able to balance this kind of lens with a sense of realism and what the person is likely to do of their own volition can end with you getting hurt by that person. The same person you may have thought you could save at one point could end up being your undoing, your new abuser. They can turn out to be someone who manipulates and uses you for a large portion of your life in the future, a portion of your life that's incredibly hard to fight your way out of. Being able to just look at everyone you meet more sensibly can be your answer. Dodging the potential for meeting a terrible and manipulative person by developing your ability to be cautious around new people instead of either blindly latching onto them or blindly avoiding them. Picking who you associate with can be a much more positive solution.

After you make that first important contact with your abuser and decide you're someone they want to keep around for their own sake, they'll initiate the second phase of their plan. This phase is often referred to as "love-bombing," the infamous phase in which the abuser showers their victims with affection and praise and essentially induces a high in the victim.

When we first enter a relationship, we enter the honeymooning phase of that relationship, in which we experience elation pretty much every time we are around that person. Our new partner is put on a pedestal in our eyes, and we can't stop thinking about them. We romanticize everything they do, right down to how they move and breathe. This first infatuation phase happens because the new partner and a new relationship introduce a lot of dopamine into our system.

TAKING CARE OF YOURSELF WORKSHEET

What are some powerful affirmations that can help you take care of yourself in this process?

Rank them between 1 to 10, where 1 is the lowest and 10 is the highest.

I am in control of my own destiny, and I am not afraid because life without them is better than death by their hand (or words).

I deserve better and so do they. Having no contact with this them will help release me from their hold on me and let them live a better life without me, too.

I am taking care of myself big time and I am facing my fear to set them free, for both of us, so that we can live the life we deserve.

They will be fine, and they don't need me to change their behavior or make them "better." They are who they are, and I accept that.

It is okay for me to grieve the loss of them in my life, but I don't have to continue living with their abuse and control.

I am no longer defined by them, and my life will continue as today I joyfully take care of myself big-time!

What are some healthy activities you can do to begin taking care of yourself?

1. ....

2. ....

3. ....

4. ....

5. ....

CONCLUSION

You Have Come a Long Way. You have endured a lot, and completing this book shows that you are committed to your recovery. Be proud of your achievements, and compliment yourself for continuing to move forward. There were probably times you wanted to give up—but you didn't—and you likely did all of this while juggling many other responsibilities in your life.

You dared to look at your life, yourself, and your pain. Excavating history is a difficult task, but the results can be life changing. Looking backwards to go forward makes sense, and I hope that has been your experience in completing the activities in this book. Once we understand where we've been and how we got there, our choices become clearer, and our paths forward become more intentional.

I request that you take some time to reflect on your experience completing this book. What are the big and small lessons you've discovered on your journey? What might you like to pass on to others? What meaning have you created from this experience?

The enduring value of uncovering our life story comes from knowing that we can recover from our pain and atone for our choices. Your recovery begins when you start looking ahead and recognizing your potential for growth and change. I urge you to continue to strive towards this process as you chart your own course in life.

The best way to continue growth is through contact with others who can understand you—whether they are friends, family members, or people who have been through similar life transitions. Let the journey to healing begin.

REFERENCES

Abused defined. (n.d.). The National Domestic Violence Hotline. https://www.thehotline.org/identify-abuse/understand-relationship-abuse/.

Brown, A. C. (2021, December). How do I turn the flying monkeys against the narcissist? Retrieved from Quora: https://www.quora.com/How-do-I-turn-the-flying-monkeys-against-the-narcissist.

care.ucdavis, b. (2021, November 10). Following Intimate Partner Violence and/or Stalking. Retrieved from care.ucdavis: https://care.ucdavis.edu/following-intimate-partner-violence-andor-stalking.

Calvete, E. (2014). Emotional abuse as a predictor of early maladaptive schemas in adolescents: Contributions to the development of depressive and social anxiety symptoms. Child abuse & neglect, 38(4), 735-746.

Crabtree, E., Wilson, C., & McElvaney, R. (2021). Childhood sexual abuse: Sibling perspectives. Journal of interpersonal violence, 36(5-6), NP3304-NP3325.

Domestic abuse may do long-term damage to women's health. (2022, June 2). Www.Heart.Org. https://www.heart.org/en/news/2020/02/17/domestic-abuse-may-do-long-term-damage-to-womens-health.

DomesticShelters.org, B. (2017, March 24). Will My Partner Be Violent After I Leave? Retrieved from DomesticShelters.org: https://www.domesticshelters.org/articles/safety-planning/will-my-partner-be-violent-after-i-leave.

Emotional and verbal abuse. (n.d.). Office on Women's Health, U.S. Department of Health and Human Services. https://www.womenshealth.gov/relationships-and-safety/other-types/emotional-and-verbal-abuse.

Forgiveness: Your Health Depends on It. (2021, November 1). Johns Hopkins Medicine. https://www.hopkinsmedicine.org/health/wellness-and-prevention/forgiveness-your-health-depends-on-it#:%7E:text=The%20good%20news%3A%20Studies%20have,of%20anxiety%2C%20depression%20and%20stress.

Focht, J. (2013, March 13). "Why Doesn't She Just Leave?" Barriers to Getting out of Abusive Relationships. Retrieved from center4research: https://www.center4research.org/doesnt-just-leave-barriers-getting-abusive-relationships/

Forms of Abuse. (2017). National Network to End Domestic Violence. https://nnedv.org/content/forms-of-abuse/.

Forray, A., & Yonkers, K. A. (2021). The collision of mental health, substance use disorder, and suicide. Obstetrics & Gynecology, 137(6), 1083-1090.

Guillen, L. (2022). Leaving an Abusive Relationship: How to Protect Yourself. Retrieved from Divorcenet: https://www.divorcenet.com/resources/divorce/leaving-abusive-relationship-how-protect-yourself.htm

Hing, N., O'Mullan, C., Mainey, L., Nuske, E., Breen, H., & Taylor, A. (2021). Impacts of male intimate partner violence on women: A life course perspective. International journal of environmental research and public health, 18(16), 8303.

Higgins, M. (2016, August 8). How To Respond When Someone Tries To Guilt You. Retrieved from bustle: https://www.bustle.com/articles/177466-5-ways-to-respond-when-someone-tries-to-guilt-trip-you.

How to Stay Safe When You're Being Stalked. (2021, July 31). Verywell Mind. https://www.verywellmind.com/stalking-what-to-do-and-how-to-stay-safe-5119465

Jacobs, M. K. (2016). awordplease. Retrieved from Escaping Your Mother, Part: III Prepare For Flying Monkeys and Healing: https://awordplease.org/2016/05/17/narcissistic-abuse-healing/amp/

Kemeny, M. E. (2003). The psychobiology of stress. Current directions in psychological science, 12(4), 124-129.

Lamoreux, K. (2021, July 21). 10 Pointers for Ending Toxic Relationships. Retrieved from psychcentral: https://psychcentral.com/blog/steps-to-end-a-toxic-relationship

Logue, B. (2019, May 11). A Shocking Response You Can Give When Someone Lashes Out at You. The Daily Positive. https://www.thedailypositive.com/a-shocking-response-you-can-give-when-someone-lashes-out-at-you/.

onelove. (2022). 11 Reasons Why People in Abusive Relationships Can't "Just Leave". Retrieved from joinonelove: https://www.joinonelove.org/learn/why_leaving_abuse_is_hard/.

Rebbe, R., Sattler, K. M., & Mienko, J. A. (2022). The association of race, ethnicity, and poverty with child maltreatment reporting. Pediatrics, 150(2).

Remschmidt, H. (2011). The emotional and neurological consequences of abuse. Dtsch Arztebl Int., 108(17):285-286. doi:10.3238/arztebl.2011.0285.

Rodgers, L. (2022, March *). How to Leave an Abusive Relationship. Retrieved from The healthy: https://www.thehealthy.com/family/rela tionships/how-to-leave-an-abusive-relationship/.

Rowntree, M. (2007). Responses to sibling sexual abuse: Are they as harmful as the abuse?. Australian Social Work, 60(3), 347-361.

Spitzberg, B.H., & Cupach, W.R. (2007). The state of the art of stalking: Taking stock of the emerging literature. Aggression and Violent Behavior, 12(1), 64-86.

Staff. (2022). WHY IT'S SO DIFFICULT TO LEAVE. Retrieved from Women Aganist Abuse: https://www.womenagainstabuse.org/educa tion-resources/learn-about-abuse/why-its-so-difficult-to-leave#:~:text=Leaving%20can%20be%20dangerous%3A%20Many.

The School of Life. (n.d.). 10 IDEAS FOR PEOPLE AFRAID TO EXIT A RELATIONSHIP. Retrieved from theschooloflife: https://www. theschooloflife.com/article/10-ideas-for-people-afraid-to-exit-a-rela tionship/.

Thompson, R.S., Bonomi, A.E., Anderson, M., Reid, R.J., Dimer, J.A., Carrell, D., & Rivara, F.P. (2006). Intimate partner violence: Prevalence, types, and chronicity in adult women. American Journal of Preventive Medicine, 30(6), 447-457.

Traumatic childhood increases lifelong risk for heart disease, early death. (2022, June 2). Www.Heart.Org. https://www.heart.org/en/news/2020/04/28/traumatic-childhood-increases-lifelong-risk-for-heart-disease-early-death.

van Heugten, K. (2021). Social work and workplace bullying, emotional abuse and harassment. Special topics and particular occupations, professions and sectors, 299-329.

violence, b. p. (2022). Intimate partner stalking, like domestic violence, is a coercive control where one person attempts to exert power over another. Retrieved from peace over violence: https://www.peaceoverviolence.org/intimate-partner-stalking.

Warriors, A. (2021). A Narcissist's Flying Monkeys + 3 Tactics To Disarm Them. Retrieved from Abuse Warriors: https://abusewarrior. com/abuse/a-narcissists-flying-monkeys/.

What Are the Different Types of Dating Abuse? (n.d.). love is respect. https://www.loveisrespect.org/is-this-abuse/types-of-abuse.

Young, K. (2017). Dealing With Difficult People. Retrieved from heysigmund: https://www.heysigmund.com/toxic-people-when-someone-you-love-toxic/comment-page-10/.